the metabolic clock

COOKBOOK

the metabolic clock

COOKBOOK

recipes to speed up your metabolism

Julie Rennie

ROCKPOOL
PUBLISHING

A Rockpool book
PO Box 252, Summer Hill
NSW 2130, Australia

www.rockpoolpublishing.com.au
www.facebook.com/RockpoolPublishing

First published in 2013

Copyright © Julie Rennie, 2013

Food Photography © Brent Parker-Jones, 2013

Printed by Everbest, China
10 9 8 7 6 5 4 3 2

National Library of Australia
Cataloguing-in-Publication entry

Rennie, Julie.

  The metabolic clock cookbook : what to eat and when to speed up your metabolism (vegetarian meals included) / Julie Rennie.

  9781921295676 (pbk.)

  Rennie, Julie. Metabolic clock ;
  2. Includes index.
  Reducing diets--Recipes.
  Metabolism--Regulation.

613.25

Edited by Jody Lee and Megan Drinan
Cover and internal design by Stan Lamond
Proofreader: Jody Lee
Food photographer: Brent Parker-Jones
Food stylist: Lee Blaylock
Food stylist assistants: Mark Hockenhull and Milli Lee

The Metabolic Clock and *The Metabolic Clock Cookbook* are designed to kickstart your journey to losing weight and gaining energy.

The author and publishers are not medical practitioners. Their intent is to offer health-related information and strategies to assist you in your journey or work with other health specialists.

We recognise that within the health, medical and fitness fields there are widely divergent viewpoints and opinions. As such, we suggest that people applying the strategies of *The Metabolic Clock* create a network of advisers that they feel can assist them with their health concerns.

The author and publishers do not prescribe that any of this material be used for the diagnosis, treatment or prescription of any illness or medical condition. If this is required, we recommend that you consult the appropriate health professionals.

The reader is responsible for their own choices in regards to their health and the implementation of any material found in *The Metabolic Clock* series.

Contents

A message from the author

It's a pleasure to present you with *The Metabolic Clock Cookbook*.

My first book, *The Metabolic Clock,* covers everything you need to know about my philosophy on losing weight and gaining energy naturally. This book includes more recipes and shows just how easy it is to create healthy, delicious food from natural ingredients. All the recipes were developed using the principles of *The Metabolic Clock* and are designed to speed up your metabolism. I really enjoyed creating these recipes and feel that I have improved my health even more with these nourishing, and often vegetarian, meals.

The recipes and way of eating and living that I suggest are far more enjoyable than a diet – and you will feel more energised as you gradually add the suggested healthy, daily practices to your life. The first practice I suggest you adopt is to actually make the time to prepare healthy food – don't you owe it to yourself to nourish your body and gain the energy to live life to the fullest?

I used to think I was too busy to cook. Then I began cooking with love and thinking about how to nourish my body. This shift in attitude has been the most important change I have made – the wellbeing that springs forth has touched every corner of my life.

Since the launch of *The Metabolic Clock* in February 2011, I have toured the country and met thousands of people at libraries, community groups, corporations and Mind–Body–Spirit events. It has been insightful for me to learn about the weight-loss and health challenges that people face today.

When I was growing up, it was rare to see an overweight kid and degenerative diseases were for the elderly. Today, there are so many options available for people to lose weight yet, as a nation, we still haven't succeeded in beating the 21st century disease of obesity. Where did we go wrong? Slowly, over many years – and in part due to our busy lifestyles – we have lost some simple health values. We are now paying the ultimate price with sluggish metabolisms, diminished health and weight gain.

Most people think that dieting is all about heavy exercise and starvation. One lady told me that if she saw another professional who told her she needed to exercise hard for one hour every day, she would punch them. She had injuries to both her knees and found walking difficult – how could she even contemplate exercise? Unfortunately, she gave up even trying to lose weight and be healthy.

Of course, there are still thousands of people who try the next diet, potion, pill or shake with moderate success for the short term. But why go to the effort of being on a diet or training hard only to revert back to the lifestyle that wasn't working for you in the first place?

Fad diets and products that promise quick weight loss can unbalance your metabolism, leaving you feeling sluggish. In order to achieve weight loss over the long term, the key is to create a healthy, balanced, daily routine that you can sustain. *The Metabolic Clock* shows you certain lifestyle changes that can make an amazing difference to your life. It guides you towards weight loss and improved health *as a way of life*.

Balance in all things.

I suggest you start with a lifestyle check-up. This will identify the practices that have become the bad habits that continually contribute to your lack of health and ultimately, weight gain. I also recommend that you read the first book, *The Metabolic Clock*. It has more recipes, meal-plans and strategies to encourage and create a healthy way of thinking.

Within the pages of *The Metabolic Clock Cookbook*, you will discover habits to stop, habits to swap and habits to start. Based on the principles of *The Metabolic Clock,* these healthy habits will speed up your metabolism so that you can lose weight easily and have more energy.

These healthy practices are a lifelong approach to your health and wellbeing. It's not about rushing in and out of a diet. It's about being consistent. By gradually incorporating these practices into your daily life, you will bring about balance within yourself *and* achieve sustainable weight loss.

I hope you enjoy these delicious recipes as much as I enjoyed creating them for you.

Julie Rennie

What is *The Metabolic Clock?*

Your metabolism is linked to nature's rhythms via your internal body clock. The daily cycle of sunrise and sunset triggers the release of hormones in the human body that manage appetite, energy, mood and sleep. However, modern living and lifestyle patterns have dramatically altered our ability to respond to nature's cues. This can result in a slow metabolism, weight gain and a general lack of energy. When you are out of sync with nature's rhythms, nothing feels right.

Think of your metabolism like a miniature sun. At sunrise it's waking up, it gathers momentum and is at its peak at midday, then it glides gently into sunset slowing down and resting. Now relate this to the modern lifestyle pattern of a late breakfast or no breakfast at all, a late lunch and a large dinner at night. With this eating pattern, you are eating most of your food during your metabolism's slowest cycle. Your body has to work hard to digest the food and you may wake up feeling very sluggish and tired.

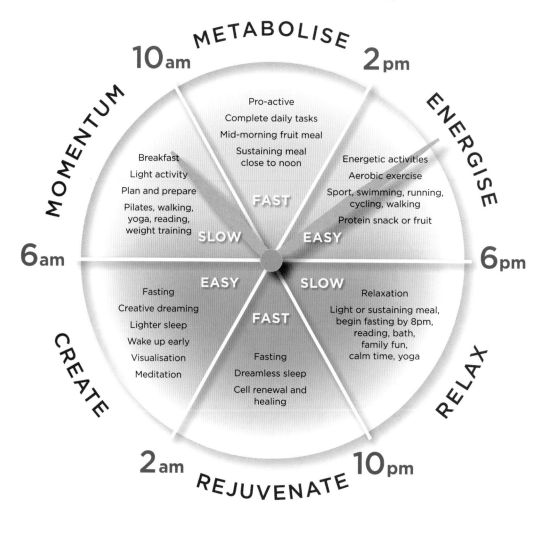

The no-diet way to a slimmer, more energised you

The Metabolic Clock shows you what to eat and when in order to speed up your metabolism and burn body fat for fuel while making it easy to shed excess kilos.

Your body requires carbohydrates to provide energy and protein and vegetables to build and repair. If you eat carbohydrates at night, when not much energy is needed, your body will store this excess energy as fat while you sleep.

On the other hand, if you go to bed without eating many carbohydrates then the reverse will happen – your body will burn fat for energy while you sleep. You can give your body the best ingredients it needs for a healing sleep with a meal of protein and vegetables in the early evening.

The six natural cycles that balance your metabolic clock

Balance your metabolic clock with the six natural cycles that manage appetite, energy, mood and sleep.

6 am to 10 am – Gaining momentum

Wake-up at sunrise and rehydrate your body. Eating breakfast cranks up the digestive furnace and gets your metabolism moving. An early breakfast will provide fuel for the day's activities.

10 am to 2 pm – Metabolising food

Eat fruit mid-morning to speed up your metabolism and fill your body with life-giving enzymes. A nourishing meal close to midday when your metabolism is most active will provide your body with the fuel it needs for an energetic afternoon.

2 pm to 6 pm – Feeling energised

If hungry, have a mid-afternoon protein snack. Do energetic exercise or walk to burn off excess fuel from the carbohydrates eaten during the day.

6 pm to 10 pm – Relaxing and winding down

Your metabolism naturally slows down at sunset so eat an early evening meal of protein and vegetables; the build and repair foods. By eliminating or minimising your carbohydrates at this time, you won't store them as body fat while you sleep. Your body also releases sleep hormones in this cycle, so get yourself to bed before 10 pm to support deep, healing sleep.

10 pm to 2 am – Rejuvenation and healing

This sleep cycle – especially the hours before midnight – rejuvenates your adrenals, balances your hormones and heals your body.

2 am to 6 am – Creative dreaming and visualisation

Have a pen and paper next to your bed to capture any creative thoughts if you wake during this dreamy sleep cycle or get up early and meditate. Choose to get up early so that your your metabolism can get moving. Sleeping late in the morning leads to feeling lethargic and slow.

Before you start

Following are some suggestions to ensure you embark on your wellness journey in the safest way possible.

Eliminating toxins

When you begin a healthy eating program and burn body fat, your body will begin to eliminate toxic substances from your system. This elimination, or detoxification, may result in headaches and a lack of energy. This is temporary and although you may feel slightly unwell, you will soon feel fantastic as the new cells will be healthier and your body won't be carrying around as many toxins.

While most people don't experience these symptoms, it's important to know that this is part of the healing process and the discomfort will vanish in a few days. The hardest thing for many people to do is to accept that they are not sick and realise that their body is cleansing itself. If this happens to you, be gentle on yourself.

Fitness safety check

Before starting on any lifestyle program it is recommended that you get a check-up with your medical practitioner to gain an idea about your current state of health. Results from your check-up will also give you something to measure your progress against. Consider this as a safety check for your body, much like the regular safety check you have done on your car. Recommended check-ups include:

- cholesterol
- blood sugar
- vitamin D
- iron
- kidney and liver function
- blood pressure
- blood type identification.

'I realised that the changes I wanted to make needed to be lifetime changes. Julie recommended that I had my blood pressure and cholesterol checked and to know my blood group. Through these checks, I discovered I had dangerously high cholesterol. The changes that I have made to my diet and how I deal with stressful situations have made a great difference to my wellbeing. I now sleep better, feel healthier and have more energy. I would not have known that my cholesterol was high without this safety check.'

— Karen

Take your measurements

Many people measure their physical shape by what they currently weigh on their bathroom scales. For some, their weigh-in results can greatly affect their whole state of mind for that day: a bad result means a bad day; a good result means a good day.

However, bathroom scales can be deceptive. The most effective form of measurement is to use a tape measure to measure each body part once a month. Ask a friend to help you record and track your measurements. The following form can be downloaded at www.metabolicclock.com.

Another way to monitor changes in your body shape is by how comfortable your clothes feel and how good you feel as you reshape your body.

It is much more inspiring to lose 50 centimetres (20 inches) of body fat than 17 kilograms (2.6 stone).

Measurements	Date __/__/____	Date __/__/____	Date __/__/____	Date __/__/____	Date __/__/____	Date __/__/____
Shoulders						
Chest						
Right arm (upper)						
Left arm (upper)						
Waist						
Hips						
Right thigh						
Left thigh						
Left calf						
Right calf						

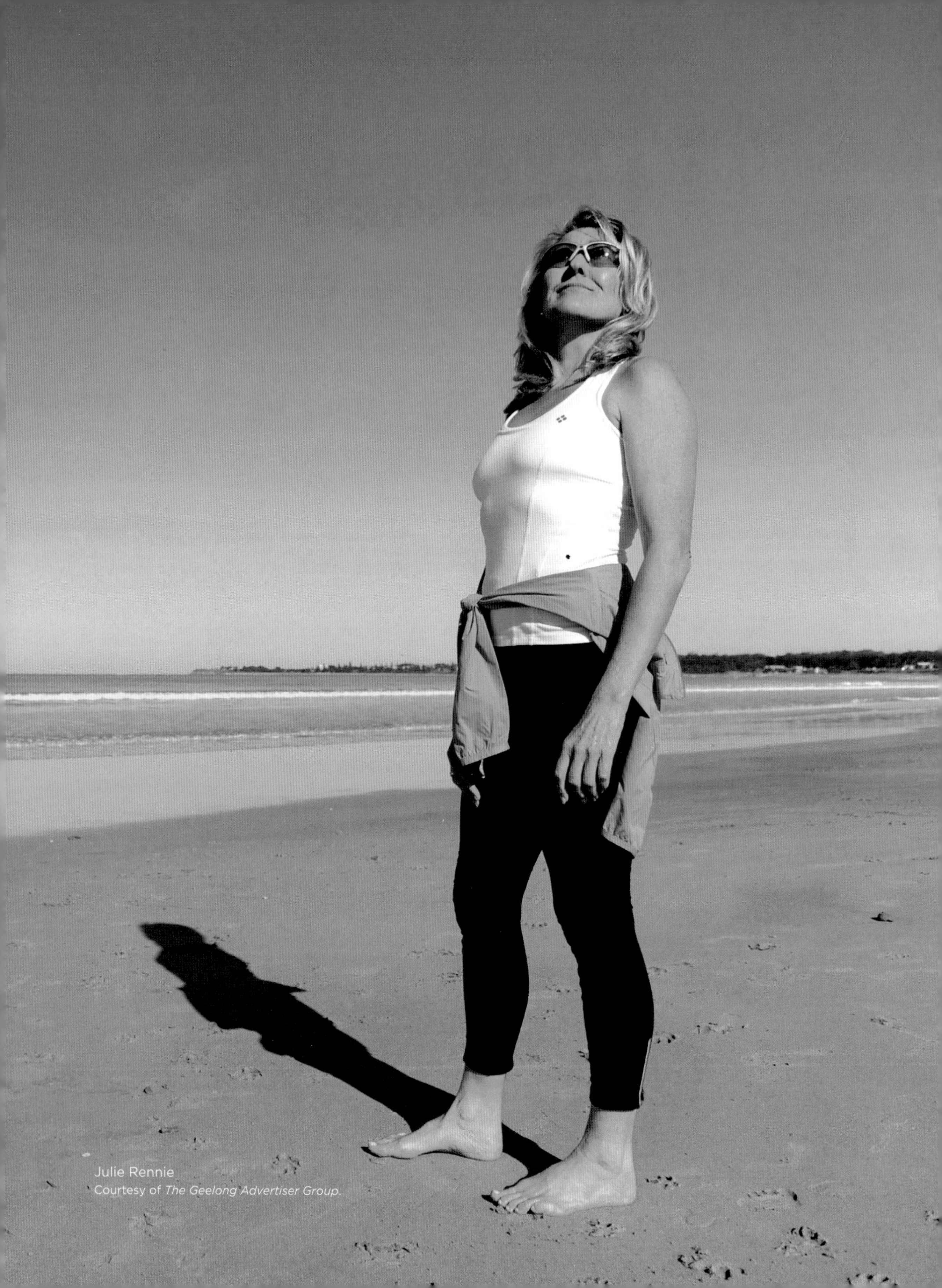

Julie Rennie
Courtesy of *The Geelong Advertiser Group.*

Lifestyle check-up

A lifestyle check-up will identify the unhealthy habits and practices that contribute to your lack of health and ultimately, weight gain.

Do you regularly skip breakfast and drink lots of tea and coffee to keep you going? Are you always putting yourself last? Do you constantly deplete your energy without nurturing and nourishing your body?

Do you skip meals to save on calories? Or do you go on fad diets, depriving yourself of nourishment? Eat on the run or rush your meals? Are you so busy that you have forgotten to allocate time to take care of your own health?

Optimum health is gained by adopting a set of healthy habits.

You can start your journey to optimum health today by simply replacing an existing habit with a more healthy one. Then choose another and keep going until being healthy feels natural to you.

On the following pages is a checklist to help you to do a review of your current daily routine. Tick the boxes of the habits that you would like to stop, the habits you would like to swap and the habits you would like to start.

The following forms can be downloaded at www.metabolicclock.com.

Habits to stop

☐ STOP EATING WHILE DRIVING, WALKING OR SITTING AT YOUR DESK

Eating in a relaxed and calm environment is good for digestion. If you eat while you are working at your desk, driving in your car or walking, you may find that you eat more food than you realise. Moreover, if you are rushing around while eating, your blood flow will go to moving muscles instead of working on the process of digestion – and your metabolism will slow down. When you relax while eating, the opposite happens and your metabolism speeds up.

☐ STOP SKIPPING MEALS AND EAT SMALLER PORTIONS REGULARLY

The digestive tract operates like a muscle – it contracts and releases while passing the food through. If you skip meals, this action stops and your metabolism slows. Eating smaller portions regularly will keep your metabolism moving in a balanced way.

☐ STOP COMPLAINING THAT YOU HAVE NO TIME FOR YOURSELF

Go to bed early and get up early. Make time for yourself at the start of the day.

☐ IF YOU ARE VEGETARIAN, DO NOT SWAP MEAT FOR CARBOHYDRATES

Choose other protein like nuts, seeds, legumes, beans, ricotta cheese, yoghurt or tofu.

☐ **STOP SHOPPING EVERY DAY FOR FOOD**

Use a meal planner for 5 days or 7 days in a row – it will save you time and money. You can also download a free meal planner at www.metabolicclock.com.

☐ **STOP DENYING YOURSELF SWEET TREATS**

For some people, limiting sweet treats can lead to cravings and bingeing. Replacing nourishing meals with these foods is not a healthy strategy, either. Have a nourishing meal first then enjoy a small treat. It will be a delight rather than a choice that leaves you feeling guilty.

☐ **STOP MICROWAVING FOOD**

Lightly steam your vegetables – microwaving destroys the enzymes in the food that are required for healthy digestion.

☐ **STOP OR MINIMISE CARBONATED DRINKS**

Did you know it takes 33 glasses of water to balance out the acidity of 1 glass of soft drink (soda)? Carbonated drinks disrupt the stomach acids needed for digestion, so view them as a treat, only having them occasionally.

☐ **STOP RUSHING AROUND**

Allow time to sit quietly every day. Get in touch with your instincts and inner peace.

☐ **STOP SNACKING AFTER YOUR EVENING MEAL**

These calories are stored as body fat while you sleep.

☐ **DON'T GO FOOD SHOPPING ON AN EMPTY STOMACH**

Eat before you go shopping. Your mind will get very excited if you are in a supermarket when you are hungry. You may find yourself grabbing a salty or sugary snack to tide you over or notice when you unpack the shopping that quite a few unhealthy foods have made their way into your shopping bags.

☐ **STOP GOING TO BED LATE**

Research has found that people who don't get enough before-midnight sleep reduce the production of the hormone leptin, the body's natural appetite suppressant. Moreover, when you are sleep deprived, your brain looks for carbohydrates. A University of Chicago study showed that sleep-deprived people ate more sweet and starchy foods – rather than protein and vegetables – resulting in weight gain.

☐ **STOP WALKING IN THE DOOR AND DUMPING STRESS ON YOUR FAMILY**

Create a pattern interrupt to release work day stress in a healthy way. Go for a brisk walk. Or better yet, take everyone for a walk.

Habits to swap

☐ **SWAP HIGHLY PROCESSED FOOD FOR FRESH FOOD**

Highly processed food has very little nutritional value. It requires a lot of energy to digest, but doesn't give you much energy in return. Fresh food, on the other hand, contains a life force that provides easily absorbed nutrients and enzymes, speeding up your metabolism. The simplest way to gain the nutrients that your body requires is to choose foods in their most natural state – they were intended to be eaten and digested in this way.

☐ **SWAP EATING CARBOHYDRATES AT NIGHT FOR CARBS DURING THE DAY**

Simply put, bread, pasta, rice and noodles are best eaten before 2 pm. If you eat carbohydrates at night, your body will store this energy as fat while you sleep because not much energy is needed at this time. If you go to bed without eating carbohydrates, the reverse will happen and your body will burn fat for energy while you sleep.

☐ **SWAP A LARGE PLATE OF FOOD AT NIGHT FOR A SMALL PLATE**

Eat more food during the day and less at night. It's not recommended that you eat a large meal at this time because sunset triggers melatonin, the relaxing hormone, which slows down your metabolism.

☐ **SWAP WHITE BREAD FOR SPELT BREAD OR MULTIGRAIN BREAD**

These breads have a lower glycaemic index, more nourishment and more fibre for your digestive system.

☐ **SWAP MIDDAY SUN FOR EARLY MORNING SUN**

Your morning dose of sunshine (before 9 am) delivers the happy hormone, serotonin, and also vitamin D – a lack of which can leave you feeling tired and depressed.

☐ **SWAP THE MORNING COFFEE FOR A FRESH, RAW JUICE OR HOT WATER WITH LEMON JUICE**

Kickstart your metabolism with a raw juice that is full of enzymes. Try half a lemon squeezed in hot water first thing in the morning as a daily detox for your body. (Lemon juice turns to alkaline ash in your digestive system, balancing high acidity levels.)

☐ **SWAP NEGATIVE DISAPPROVING THOUGHTS FOR EMPOWERING THOUGHTS**

Create an interruption to your thinking when nagging, negative thoughts begin to take hold. Say to yourself, 'Stop!' and choose a more empowering thought.

☐ **SWAP POTATOES FOR PUMPKIN AND SWEET POTATOES**

They have a lower glycaemic index.

☐ **SWAP FROZEN VEGETABLES FOR FRESH VEGETABLES**

Fresh vegetables contain live enzymes that spark your metabolism, helping it to move faster.

SWAP BLENDED VEGETABLE OIL FOR COLD-PRESSED OLIVE OIL

Olive oil is a high-quality, essential fatty acid.

 SWAP TEA AND COFFEE FOR HERBAL TEA AT NIGHT

Try chamomile tea instead. Reducing caffeine aids restful sleep and overall wellness.

 SWAP CAKES MADE FROM WHITE FLOUR FOR CAKES MADE FROM ALMOND MEAL, RICOTTA CHEESE OR SPELT FLOUR

These ingredients are more nourishing.

 SWAP RICE FOR QUINOA GRAIN

Quinoa grain has a high protein content and is therefore more nourishing.

SWAP PROCESSED SALT FOR CELTIC SEA SALT

Celtic sea salt is mineral-rich and has lots of flavour. It is free of any processing which helps lock in many vital trace elements.

 **SWAP HIGH GI FOODS FOR LOW GI FOODS**

Low GI carbohydrates are absorbed slowly into your system, meaning you get a steady flow of energy. You will also feel more balanced and put less stress on your pancreas.

SWAP CLUTTER WITH REGULAR TIDY-UPS

Gain agreement from everyone in your household to do a 5-minute clean up every day. If there are four people in your household and you all stop what you are doing and clean up for five minutes, that is a 20-minute clean that has been shared! This could include putting washing away, sorting the coffee table, putting dirty clothes in the laundry etc. Put music on and make it fun for everyone.

Habits to start

 EAT SOME RAW FOOD EVERY DAY

The enzymes in raw food act like spark plugs, firing up many healing processes within your body. So eat raw food whenever you eat cooked food – it could be as simple as putting fresh raw herbs over your cooked food. This will give you the enzymes needed to digest the cooked food more quickly, speeding up your metabolism.

BOOK YOUR TRAINING TIMES INTO YOUR DIARY

This single activity makes a big difference. There will always be a distraction not to train. You are essentially making an appointment with yourself just as you would with any other person. Book all other appointments around your training times.

NOT SURE HOW MUCH WATER TO DRINK?

Fill a 1-litre (2 pints) bottle and carry it with you.

FEEL LIKE GIVING UP ON YOUR GOOD HABITS?

Remind yourself of the compelling reasons to keep going. Having them written down somewhere helps too.

 IF A GOAL SEEMS OUT OF REACH, CREATE MINI GOALS

A big goal is achieved with many daily activity goals – focus on the daily goals.

 PLAN YOUR MEALS AHEAD OF TIME

Think about what you are going to have for dinner in the morning – not at night.

SIT IN THE DARK BEFORE GOING TO BED

The absence of light triggers the release of melatonin. This sleep hormone relaxes you and prepares you for a deep, healing sleep.

 START TAKING A PROBIOTIC SUPPLEMENT

This will boost the healthy bacteria in your digestive tract and aid digestion.

 WALK BAREFOOT ON THE LAWN OR BEACH

Get healing vibes from the ground. The Earth is a large battery that is charged by the sun. When you walk barefoot on the Earth you are absorbing electrons brimming with higher energy.

 DRINK WATER BETWEEN MEALS RATHER THAN WITH YOUR MEALS

Water dilutes the stomach acid required to break down the hard protein coating around certain foods. Keep your stomach acid level high at mealtimes and drink your water between meals.

MOVE YOUR BODY TO HAVE FUN

You could adopt some playful activities like riding bikes with your kids, walking the dog, play wrestle with your kids, shoot hoops, have a hit of tennis or join a sporting club. Any of these activities will energise you and create a happy state of being.

MOVE YOUR BODY TO HAVE A HEALTHY IMMUNE SYSTEM

The lymph system, or immune system, has no pump or beat of its own so needs movement to activate it and circulate the toxins. Exercise – even the simple act of walking – will get this process working.

MOVE YOUR BODY TO CHANGE HOW YOU FEEL ABOUT YOURSELF

Approach moving your body or exercising first as a way to feel good and *then* to look good. It's a quick way to change your emotional state, which helps you to make healthy choices.

BUY SOME NEW WORKOUT CLOTHES

This will make you feel like you want to put them on and will help motivate you.

BE MINDFUL

Before you eat anything, ask the question, 'Is this going to nourish me?'

 THE NEXT TIME YOU ARE CRAVING SUGARY OR STARCHY FOOD, EAT SOME PROTEIN

Your body may be undernourished. Eating protein stops you from feeling hungry.

 TO AID DIGESTION, EAT YOUR FOOD VERY SLOWLY AND CHEW YOUR FOOD THOROUGHLY BEFORE SWALLOWING

Try putting your knife and fork down between mouthfuls. Remind yourself to eat slowly.

 PAY ATTENTION TO YOUR INSTINCTS

If you are eating something and it is making you feel uncomfortable, pay attention to the signs and stop eating it.

 SIT QUIETLY FOR 5 MINUTES OR MORE AFTER EATING

This allows more energy to be focused on digestion. A relaxed digestive system is more efficient.

 EAT LOTS OF NATURAL, FIBRE-RICH FOODS DAILY

The good bacteria in your digestive system require feeding. They thrive on vegetables, especially green leaves, fruit, nuts, seeds and whole grains. Fibre-rich foods provide a workout for your colon. In other words, it's the exercise program that doesn't raise a sweat.

Finding it hard? Make an agreement with yourself ...

Finally, if you can't give up a bad habit, minimise it. Do less of it.

A strategy that works is to create supporting agreements. These are agreements you make with yourself that will help you minimise a bad habit. Some examples of supporting agreements include:

I have three alcohol-free days each week.

I stop eating before I feel full.

I always sit down to eat.

I always carry a water bottle with me.

I eat some raw food every day.

I eat breakfast every day.

Jenny used supporting agreements to minimise her stimulant pattern of eight cups of coffee a day. She had unsuccessfully tried to give up drinking coffee many times. She recognised that it would be good for her overall health to stop drinking coffee, but she had certain attachments to the taste and aroma and also loved the social aspect of going out with friends for a coffee.

Her coffee intake was, however, causing an imbalance as she was using coffee as a morning kickstart or a pick-me-up if she was stressed or tired. She decided it would be easier to minimise it rather than try to give it up completely. Jenny made the commitment to minimise coffee in a series of supporting agreements. Her first challenge was to minimise the 8 coffees a day.

Supporting agreement number 1: *I do not drink instant coffee.*

Supporting agreement number 2: *I only drink freshly brewed coffee.*

Supporting agreement number 3: *I do not drink coffee after 4 pm.*

For 21 days, Jenny kept to her agreements. The result was that Jenny dramatically reduced her coffee intake. She felt more in control of her choices and gained a sense of achievement. Although she had not given up coffee completely, she had gained momentum towards giving it up. So a new agreement was added.

Supporting agreement number 4: *I only have one cup of coffee a day.*

Jenny chose this cup of coffee to be in the morning as she still felt she needed a kickstart in the morning. She completed this challenge and felt really proud. She had reduced 8 cups of coffee a day to just one cup a day. Her supporting agreements kept her on track. Over time, Jenny realised that even the morning coffee was stimulant-driven as she felt that she relied on it. This left her feeling incomplete about her challenge. So she added another new agreement.

Supporting agreement number 5: *I will not have a coffee until I have had a fresh, raw juice and eaten breakfast.*

The first three mornings were the most challenging for Jenny. After that, she was surprised at how much clearer her head was from giving up her morning coffee – the fresh, raw juice actually gave her a bigger lift than the coffee. These days, Jenny rarely thinks about coffee. She is in control of this choice now and occasionally enjoys a coffee with friends.

Nature's power foods for weight loss

Nature has provided so many wonderful natural foods, each with their own unique nutritional benefits. The following list highlights a few that are nature's power foods for weight loss. They are readily available and can be easily included in your daily meals.

APPLES
Apples stimulate the digestive system and cleanse it by eliminating toxins from the small intestine. The pectin in apples – especially in green Granny Smiths – slows the rise in blood sugar, reduces the build up of arterial plaque and promotes proper protein digestion. The alkaline elements of apples increase the flow of saliva for carbohydrate digestion.

ALMONDS
Almonds are the perfect alkalising protein. The good fats in almonds reduce cholesterol levels and decrease the risk of heart disease. Other properties in almonds improve memory and concentration, help the nerves to relax, provide calcium and assist with fat metabolism.

BERRIES
All berries have their special qualities and when you put strawberries, blueberries and raspberries together, you have a fruit mix full of antioxidants, vitamin C, iron and enzymes with anti-inflammatory qualities.

BRAZIL NUTS
Brazil nuts are rich in the mineral selenium, which is vital for diabetics because it stimulates glucose absorption. These nuts have a remarkable supply of amino acids, making them a complete protein source. They also have a good supply of calcium.

CELERY
This amazing vegetable has cholesterol-lowering properties and can decrease blood pressure. Celery juice can prevent hardened arteries and naturally thins the blood. It reduces the pain of arthritis and rheumatism. Celery is a good food source for diabetics because it stimulates the pancreas glands, producing insulin for carbohydrate digestion.

CARROT
Carrot juice is great for cleansing the liver. Carrots are a rich source of carotene, which the body converts into vitamin A. This vitamin is required to promote the secretion of the gastric juices required for protein digestion.

CHERRIES
Cherries have a very low GI, which makes them an ideal fruit for diabetics. Cherries provide melatonin, the hormone that relaxes and promotes sleep. They have pain-killing power and can assist with the pain of headaches, gout and arthritis because they retard the enzymes that cause tissue inflammation.

CHIA SEEDS
These amazing seeds will nourish you and make you feel full. They contain high amounts of omega 3 essential fatty acids and are high in protein and calcium. They are high in soluble fibre and also boost your metabolic rate. Mix a teaspoon of seeds in a glass of water and drink.

LEMONS

Lemons are packed with vitamin C and provide an alkaline balance while cleansing the digestive system. Lemons reduce uric acid in conditions such as gout, rheumatism and gallstones. Half a lemon squeezed into hot water is a simple way to detoxify your body.

LINSEEDS

Linseeds have more essential fatty acids than fish. The omega 3 fatty acids prevent the build-up of toxic biochemicals that the body produces under stress. The essential fatty acids benefit the heart by lowering bad cholesterol. This lowers the probability of clots in the arteries, which may lead to stroke and heart attack. Linseeds are also an excellent source of dietary fibre.

PARSLEY

Parsley is a rich source of vitamins A and C. It supports the immune system by providing antioxidants that clean up the blood. It's also a rich source of iron that builds up the blood. Add chopped parsley to salads and cooked foods.

PINEAPPLE

Pineapple is a natural blood thinner. It also contains an enzyme called bromelain, which helps the pancreas produce the chemicals that digest protein, fats and carbohydrates. The anti-inflammatory properties of pineapple can also assist with easing the symptoms of gout and rheumatoid arthritis.

ROLLED OATS

Oats are good news for diabetics because they contain manganese, which helps stabilise glucose levels. It has good iron content and when you add mixed berries to your muesli, the vitamin C content of the berries assists in the absorption of the iron. Oats contain a special ingredient in the fibre called beta glucan, which slows the rise in blood sugar levels and reduces blood cholesterol.

SESAME SEEDS

The calcium content of sesame seeds is excellent, making them an ideal non-dairy calcium food. Sesame seeds inhibit the absorption of cholesterol and assist with controlling blood sugar levels for diabetics. They also assist with inflammation from rheumatoid arthritis and are an excellent supply of iron and protein.

SUNFLOWER SEEDS

Sunflower seeds absorb a lot of the sun's energy. They are rich in vitamin E, which protects from ageing and skin cell damage. They are an excellent source of good fats and are a complete protein.

WALNUTS

Walnuts are a valuable supply of omega 3 essential fatty acids and iron. The minerals in walnuts make them a great brain food. They also contain melatonin, which promotes restful sleep. Chop up a handful of walnuts to have with your evening salad or steamed vegetables.

Incidental exercise

The most important formula of *The Metabolic Clock* is to focus on what to eat and when, according to nature's energy cycles. When it comes to weight loss, the amount of carbohydrates you eat for energy needs to be used up in a day or this fuel will be stored as body fat while you sleep.

So, if you have body fat that you are unhappy about, an empowering perspective is to view body fat as excess energy waiting to be used. One way to burn off body fat is to eat fewer carbohydrates, especially of an evening, so that the fat stores will be converted into fuel.

You can also do more incidental exercise that requires energy so that your body starts to burn the body fat in response to the extra activity. Incidental exercise for our ancestors was normal as they rode horses to work, walked long distances and laboured in their backyard to grow their own food. Our modern day lifestyles have eliminated these incidental activities, which has given rise to the introduction of health clubs for structured exercise.

It's very easy to add incidental exercise and it can be a lot of fun. Try the following incidental exercise:

1. Walk the dog every day.
2. Shoot hoops with the kids.
3. If listening to music, crack into a dance.
4. Get off public transport and walk for part of the journey.
5. Take the stairs.
6. Feeling stressed? Go for a walk.
7. Do some leg squats while watching the cake cook.
8. When driving in your car, pull in your stomach muscles and move your torso from side to side to give your core muscles a workout. Do 10 sets of 10.
9. Feeling excited about something? Run on the spot for a few seconds.
10. Put the remotes away so you have to get up to change the channel.
11. Play wrestle with your kids.
12. Play Wii sports games or games like Twister.
13. Mow the lawn yourself.
14. Laugh louder. Laugh with your whole body.
15. Move with enthusiasm.

Once you reach your ideal weight, you may find that it fluctuates slightly depending on the amount of carbohydrates you eat and when you eat them. If you begin to eat more carbohydrates, you may notice that you put on body fat. You will be able to easily balance your weight by reducing the carbohydrates you eat, especially at night, and increasing incidental exercise.

Cooking with love and purpose

Most people only think about food when they are hungry or from the perspective of their next meal. With this approach, you may not gain all the nourishment required to fuel your body efficiently. Instead, if you look at your nourishment requirements over the 24 hours in a day, you will have more balanced energy levels to perform all activities comfortably and easily.

Added to this, our natural food system has been altered by over-processing, which strips vital nutrients from the raw ingredients. My intention in writing this book is to encourage you to get back to enjoying foods in their natural state and prepare meals without using processed food. When planning your meals, ensure that you include good quality protein, lots of plant food, low GI carbohydrates and essential fatty acids every day.

Protein is the building block your body uses to build the cells that create muscle, organs, skin, hair and nails. Calcium can also be found in many protein foods. When you eat protein, your body is satiated and sends signals to your gut to dull your appetite. This leaves you feeling satisfied instead of hungry.

The vegetarian recipes in this book all contain non-meat protein. The vegetarian recipes are listed at the beginning of each section. Non-vegetarians will also enjoy the vegetarian options.

Milk is a complete source of protein and calcium, however many people do not have the digestive enzymes present in their stomach to curdle the milk, which is how it is digested. For this reason, I recommend the curdled milk products of yoghurt and ricotta cheese. These contain the probiotics that aid digestion while providing nourishment. You can also experiment with goat's feta. If you have known food allergies to these foods, then do not use in the following recipes.

Include lots of plant food, particularly fruit and vegetables that are rich in vitamins and minerals. When you eat vegetables as part of your evening meal you provide your body with the antioxidants needed to clean up toxins in the body. These antioxidants go to work when you sleep.

Eating vegetables at night also provides fibre, assisting your digestive system to do some cleaning while you relax during sleep. When eaten raw, they provide the life-giving enzymes that fire off many chemical reactions needed for the body's functions. The evening meals in this book all include plant food.

The Glycaemic Index (GI) is a measurement of how fast the carbohydrates in a food enters your bloodstream, resulting in a boost in blood sugar levels. When you choose carbohydrates with a low glycaemic index, the sugar or energy of the food enters your blood steam at a slow rate. The slow absorption from low GI carbohydrates means that you get a steady flow of energy and feel more balanced. Low GI carbohydrates have been used in most of the following recipes.

While potatoes and bananas are plant foods, they are not used very often in *The Metabolic Clock* because they have a high GI. I have included potato as a treat in three of the midday meals. This will give you the opportunity to burn off the carbohydrates in the afternoon.

For many years, I wanted to remove wheat flour from my diet but wasn't organised enough to actually do it. Finally, I flicked the switch in my mind and have replaced wheat flour in my recipes with spelt flour. To my surprise, spelt flour is really flavoursome and filling. Spelt flour has a high-protein content, provides more vitamins and minerals than wheat flour and has a satisfying, nutty taste.

In ancient times, bread was a real staple in our diet. This was before the over-processing of wheat flour. I believe that part of the weight problems we are experiencing today are due to the empty calories in our foods made from wheat. When the body isn't nourished, it craves more food. We then eat more to satisfy our lack of nourishment – not our hunger.

It's ironic that essential fatty acids – commonly called good fats – balance out the bad fats. The good fats help prevent clogging of the arteries and lower bad cholesterol. Good fat will also moisten your digestive system. Eating a low-fat diet is hard to maintain because low-fat foods just don't satisfy. Good fats provide a concentrated source of energy in the diet and also satisfies the appetite. Many of the following recipes include the good fats.

If you are a person who enjoys a treat, don't deny yourself and get out of balance. When you focus on nourishing your body, a sweet treat becomes a delight rather than a choice that will leave you feeling guilty. The treats in this section are all made with some nourishing ingredients. The protein in the treat recipes is filling and you won't eat too much of it.

The Kitchen Helpers section gives you basic recipes that are the foundation to creating many nourishing meals. They also save you time and money and add depth and flavour to your meals. Make a few of them once a week. Maximise the use of your oven when baking and roast a batch of pumpkin which can later be added to a salad. Or, roast a garlic bulb or beetroot for other meals.

The recipes are listed for the right time of day to eat your carbohydrates and protein, taking the guesswork out for you. Experiment with the recipes. If you do not like an ingredient, replace it with something that you do like. When you cook with a variety of natural ingredients, each provides different vitamins and minerals essential to optimal health.

Portion size of meals is an important factor not only in terms of weight management but also your health – if you overeat, you will overwhelm your digestive system. When anything is overwhelmed, its capacity to perform well diminishes. The meals are created on the premise of eating smaller portions more regularly. It may be necessary for you to adjust to smaller portions, but you will notice how much lighter it will make you feel.

Finally, be excited and passionate about creating healthy food for yourself and your family. Cooking is a lot more enjoyable with this attitude.

Get your kitchen organised

A little bit of planning in your kitchen will save you time and money. You can start by cleaning out your pantry. Throw out any out-of-date or unhealthy foods. Re-stock with the basic ingredients from the recipes in this book. When your pantry is stocked with healthy ingredients, you simply need to shop for fresh food.

Next, clean out your refrigerator. Remove the crisper and replace it with a variety of different-sized plastic containers. Store fresh vegetables in these containers. They will keep their freshness for longer and will be much easier to find. No more rummaging around the bottom of the crisper.

Start planning your meals for 5 to 7 days at a time. Then make a shopping list before you go shopping or order the food online and have it delivered. The following shopping lists include all the ingredients from the recipes in this book. You can also download them from www.metabolicclock.com.

Many of the ingredients are readily available in supermarkets or health food stores.

- You can make your own preserved lemons from the recipe in the Kitchen Helpers section or you will find ready-made jars in specialty or gourmet food stores. It is very important to sterilise your preserving jars so that any unwelcome bacteria are destroyed before you fill your jars with food. To do this, thoroughly wash your glass jars and lids and leave to drip-dry. When dry, place the jars upright on a baking tray. Heat the oven to 50°C (120°F) and place the tray of jars in the oven for 20 minutes. The lids can be boiled in a pot of hot water for 20 minutes and removed with a pair of tongs. Drip-dry the lids on a clean tea towel.

- Tamari is a healthier version of soy sauce. I have found it in some supermarkets and most health food stores.

- Mirin, a kind of rice wine, is a Japanese condiment found in some supermarkets and Asian grocers.

- Celtic sea salt – unprocessed and full of minerals and trace elements – is found in health food stores.

- Spelt flour is found in some supermarkets and most health food stores. In Australia, the Simply No Knead spelt flour and bread improver is excellent. For suppliers near you, go to www.snk.com.au.

- Baking with spelt flour and almond meal creates a denser texture and it can create quite a sticky mix, however it bakes just fine and tastes yummy.

- You can choose to use tinned beans or cook your own dried beans in some of the recipes. Make sure you drain and wash tinned beans. Of course, there is more nourishment from soaking and cooking dried beans yourself. Whichever beans you use, do not salt the water when cooking because it toughens the skin.

- I buy parmesan cheese in a small block and cut it into chunks then shred in a food processer. This is a lot quicker than grating it. It stores in an airtight container in the refrigerator for a couple of weeks.

- Oats are so nourishing that I often process them into breadcrumbs to use in biscuit bases. This adds more fibre to the recipe.

Basic pantry shopping list

- allspice
- almond meal
- almonds
- almonds, flaked
- apple juice, organic
- apricot fruit spread
- baking powder
- balsamic vinegar
- bamboo skewers
- bay leaves
- blueberries, frozen
- borlotti beans, dried
- brazil nuts
- bread for wraps (flat/pocket/Mexican bread)
- bread improver
- bread, spelt or multigrain
- butter (lima) beans, dried
- butter (lima) beans, tin
- cannellini beans, dried
- cannellini beans, tin
- Celtic sea salt
- chickpeas (garbanzo), tin
- chilli powder

- Chinese five spice
- chocolate, dark for cooking
- cinnamon sticks
- cloves
- cocoa powder, Dutch
- coriander, (cilantro) ground
- cumin, ground
- currants
- dates, dried
- Dijon mustard
- fennel seeds
- fish sauce
- garam masala
- honey (manuka or cold extracted)
- hot paprika
- linseeds
- macadamia nuts
- maple syrup, pure
- marsala, dry
- mirin
- miso
- muslin and string for herb bags
- nori, dried seaweed

- olive oil, lemon-flavoured
- olive oil, preferably cold pressed
- olives, baby
- olives, kalamata
- oregano, dried
- oven baking bags
- peas, frozen
- pepita seeds
- peppercorns, for pepper mill
- pistachios
- pitted cherries, jar
- preserved lemons
- prunes, pitted
- quinoa
- raisins
- red curry paste, jar
- red kidney beans, tin
- red lentils
- rice flour
- rice paper wrappers
- rice vinegar
- rolled oats
- sesame seeds
- spelt flour, white

- spelt flour, wholemeal
- sprouting seeds (alfalfa, radish, red clover, chickpea (garbanzo))
- stock, beef
- stock, chicken
- stock, vegetable
- sugar, icing (powdered)
- sugar, raw caster
- sumac
- sun-dried tomatoes
- sunflower seeds
- sweet paprika
- tahini
- tamari
- Thai red curry paste
- tomato paste
- tomatoes diced, tin
- tuna, tin
- vanilla beans/vanilla essence
- walnuts
- white vinegar
- wine, dry red
- wine, dry white
- yeast, dried

Fresh food shopping list

MEAT

- [ ] bacon, middle rashers
- [ ] beef, corned
- [ ] beef, lean minced
- [ ] beef, pot roast
- [ ] chicken, breast
- [ ] chicken, thighs/drumsticks
- [ ] chicken, whole
- [ ] fish, snapper or red mullet
- [ ] lamb, backstrap or steak
- [ ] lamb, cutlets
- [ ] lamb, shanks
- [ ] osso bucco steak
- [ ] salmon, steak
- [ ] seafood marinara mix
- [ ] squid hoods
- [ ] steak, eye fillet
- [ ] steak, porterhouse
- [ ] steak, rump

SUNDRY

- [ ] bocconcini
- [ ] butter
- [ ] buttermilk
- [ ] eggs, free-range or organic
- [ ] feta cheese
- [ ] goat's feta, marinated
- [ ] haloumi or kefalograviera cheese
- [ ] milk, organic
- [ ] parmesan cheese, grated and whole
- [ ] ricotta, fresh
- [ ] tofu
- [ ] yoghurt, Greek
- [ ] yoghurt, natural (preferably biodynamic)

FRUIT & VEGETABLES

- [ ] apricots
- [ ] Asian basil leaves
- [ ] asparagus
- [ ] avocado
- [ ] basil
- [ ] bay leaves
- [ ] bean sprouts
- [ ] beetroot (beet)
- [ ] blueberries
- [ ] bok choy
- [ ] borlotti beans
- [ ] broad (fava) beans
- [ ] broccolini (baby broccoli)
- [ ] capsicum (peppers), red and green
- [ ] carrot
- [ ] celery
- [ ] cherries
- [ ] chillies, red
- [ ] Chinese cabbage
- [ ] coriander (cilantro)
- [ ] cucumber, Lebanese
- [ ] dates, fresh
- [ ] eggplant (aubergine), large
- [ ] eggplant (aubergine), oriental
- [ ] fennel bulb
- [ ] fig
- [ ] garlic
- [ ] ginger
- [ ] grapes
- [ ] green apples
- [ ] green beans
- [ ] kale (Tuscan cabbage)
- [ ] kiwifruit
- [ ] leek
- [ ] lemongrass stalk
- [ ] lemons
- [ ] lettuce, butter
- [ ] lettuce, cos (romaine)
- [ ] lettuce, iceberg
- [ ] limes
- [ ] mandarins
- [ ] mango
- [ ] mint
- [ ] mint, Vietnamese
- [ ] mushrooms, assorted
- [ ] mushrooms, button
- [ ] mushrooms, large
- [ ] nectarines
- [ ] onions, brown
- [ ] onions, pickling
- [ ] oranges
- [ ] oregano, fresh
- [ ] parsley, flat-leaf
- [ ] passionfruit
- [ ] pea pods
- [ ] peaches
- [ ] pears
- [ ] pineapple
- [ ] potato
- [ ] pumpkin, Jap
- [ ] raspberries
- [ ] red cabbage
- [ ] rocket leaves (arugula)
- [ ] rosemary
- [ ] salad leaves, mixed
- [ ] Spanish onions
- [ ] spinach leaves, English and baby
- [ ] spring onions
- [ ] sprouts, mixed
- [ ] strawberries
- [ ] sugar snap peas
- [ ] sweet potato
- [ ] thyme
- [ ] tomatoes, cherry
- [ ] tomatoes, large
- [ ] tomatoes, Roma
- [ ] watercress
- [ ] zucchini (courgette)

The *Metabolic Clock* Daily Recipes

The following recipes are everyday meals designed for busy people who want to enjoy food in its most natural and nourishing state.

- If you have any food allergies, just make adjustments to the ingredients.

- If you do not want to try spelt flour then use any other flour. This will be an experiment for you.

- Each recipe specifies the number of meals it makes.

- Each recipe can easily be doubled or multiplied depending on the number of meals required.

- Some recipes allow for leftovers or for portions to be frozen for another meal.

CONVERSION NOTE FOR MEASURES

One Australian metric measuring cup holds approximately 250ml (8 oz); one Australian metric tablespoon holds 20ml (just under 1 oz); one Australian metric teaspoon holds 5ml (⅙ oz).

The difference between one country's measuring cups and another's is within a two- or three-teaspoon variance, and will not affect your cooking results. North America, New Zealand and the United Kingdom use a 15ml (½ oz) tablespoon.

Opposite page: Green vegetable medley

Kitchen helpers

These simple recipes help you to add flavour and variety to meals. They do not take long to make and can be shared across many meals. They help you to make a meal tasty and delicious in very little time. I like to make a few on shopping day.

- Rosemary flavour bag
- Favourite spice mix
- Sprouted seeds
- Sweet chilli sauce
- Mustard and orange salad dressing
- Lemon mayonnaise
- Roasted garlic bulbs
- Spelt chapatti
- Roasted pumpkin, two ways
- Yoghurt cheese balls

- Ratatouille
- Four easy salads
- Homemade yoghurt
- Preserved lemons
- Basic roast chicken
- Green vegetable medley
- Homemade tomato sauce
- Spelt bread
- Homemade muesli
- Cooked quinoa

Rosemary flavour bag

Rosemary is easy to grow in your garden or in a pot. It adds a rich flavour to stews and soups. The leaves can become tough when cooked and not pleasant to eat so that is why I like to tie them in muslin. These flavour pouches can then be placed in your cooking pots and removed at the end of the cooking.

1 sprig fresh rosemary
muslin
cooking string

Cut out 8 cm x 8 cm (3 in x 3 in) squares of muslin. Fill with rosemary stems and tie with string.

Favourite spice mix

Mix together the following spices and place in an airtight jar. Use the mix to flavour soups and stews or as a rub on meat.

4 tablespoons dried coriander (cilantro)
4 tablespoons ground cumin
2 tablespoons garam masala
2 tablespoons sweet paprika

Opposite page:
Rosemary flavour bag

Sprouted seeds

Sprouted foods are one of the best sources of living enzymes, which increase your metabolism. When a seed is given water and sunlight, elements contained in the seed are quickly converted to provide energy. At this early stage of growth there is a high quality of nutrients that are easy to digest.

Increase your metabolism by adding sprouts to your salads and sandwiches. Alfalfa, buckwheat, radish, red clover, lentil, chickpeas (garbanzo), mung bean and sunflower seeds are the most common sprouts. Purchase organic seeds for a healthier sprout.

> 1 tablespoon mixed red clover, radish and alfalfa seeds
> 1 glass jar
> 1 piece muslin
> 1 rubber band

Place seeds in jar. Fill the jar to half way with cold water. Place the muslin over the rim of the jar and fix in place with a rubber band. Tip the jar upside down over a sink to drain the water. This washes the seeds. Refill the jar half way up with water.

Place on a windowsill or a light-filled part of your kitchen. Leave to soak for 24 hours. The water and light will kickstart your seeds into life. After 24 hours, tip the jar upside down over the sink and drain out the water.

Refill with water and drain all water out twice a day for 4 to 6 days.

When seeds begin to throw off their hulls, fill the jar with water and remove the muslin cover. Tip out just enough water to take out the hulls that are floating on the surface. Place the muslin on the jar and fix in place with the rubber band. Drain again. Lay the jar horizontally so there is more surface area for sprouts to grow.

The sprouts are ready to eat in 7 days. Store in an airtight container in the refrigerator. They will keep fresh for 3 to 4 days. Start another jar of seeds growing.

NOTE: Specially designed sprouting jars are available from health food stores.

Sweet chilli sauce

2 garlic cloves, peeled and crushed
6 large red chillies
1/2 teaspoon fish sauce
1 cup rice vinegar
1/2 cup water
3 tablespoons raw caster sugar

Grind the garlic and chilli in a mortar and pestle or food processor. Place in a small saucepan over medium heat with all the other ingredients and simmer for 20 minutes or until a little sticky. Cool slightly and place in a sterilised jar (see page 28 for instructions). Store in the refrigerator.

NOTE: For a milder sauce, de-seed 3 of the chillies. The heat is in the seeds.

Mustard and orange salad dressing

1 heaped teaspoon Dijon mustard
1/2 cup fresh orange juice
1/4 cup olive oil
1 teaspoon manuka honey
pinch of Celtic sea salt
cracked black pepper

Place mustard, orange juice, oil and honey in a jar with a tight-fitting lid. Shake to combine then season to taste with Celtic salt and pepper. Store in refrigerator.

Lemon mayonnaise

1 free-range or organic egg, yolk only
1/2 teaspoon Dijon mustard
2 teaspoons lemon juice
100 ml (3 1/2 fl oz) olive oil
1/2 teaspoon manuka honey
1/2 teaspoon finely grated lemon zest

Whisk the egg yolk, mustard and lemon juice in a small bowl. Add the oil slowly, a couple of drops at a time while whisking until the mayonnaise thickens. Stir through the honey and lemon zest. Place in a glass jar and store in the refrigerator for up to a week.

Roasted garlic bulbs

Roasted garlic has a sweeter, richer flavour than raw garlic. Boost the flavour of dips, dressings, stews and soups or spread on toasted bread and top with tomato slices.

2 bulbs garlic
olive oil, to drizzle

Peel away the outer skins of the bulbs. Cut the heads off the top of the bulbs to expose each garlic clove. Drizzle with olive oil and place in a muffin tin. Cover with foil and bake. For firmer cloves, bake for 35 minutes. If you like a softer bulb, bake for 45 minutes. When cool, place in an airtight container and store in the refrigerator for up to 2 weeks.

Opposite page:
Roasted garlic bulbs

Spelt chapatti

These flat breads are a great accompaniment to a curry or a stew.
Use instead of rice.

Makes 4

½ cup white spelt flour
½ cup wholemeal spelt flour
½ teaspoon Celtic sea salt
¼ teaspoon ground cumin
½ cup lukewarm water

Sift the flours together into a medium-sized bowl and add the Celtic
salt and cumin. Make a well in the middle and gradually add the
water, mixing well with a wooden spoon or using your fingers. Add
enough water to form a soft dough. Turn the dough onto a lightly
floured surface and knead for about 5 minutes. Wrap in plastic and
place in the refrigerator for 15 minutes.

Divide the dough into 4 equal portions. On a lightly floured surface,
roll each piece into a circle. Place a heavy based, non-stick frying
pan over high heat. When the pan is hot, reduce the heat to medium
and dry fry the first chapatti turning over once when the chapatti
begins to bubble. If the pan is hot it may only take 1 minute on
each side.

Remove the cooked chapatti from the pan and cover with foil to
keep warm. Repeat the process until all the breads are cooked. Serve
immediately with a meal or allow to cool and store in the freezer in a
sealed plastic bag. To re-use once unfrozen, dry fry in a heavy frying
pan over high heat.

Roasted pumpkin, two ways

When cooled, the pumpkin can be stored in the refrigerator and used in salads and wraps or reheated to add to a meal. Sweet potato can also be used.

Spiced pumpkin

¼ Jap pumpkin, peeled and cut into 3 cm (1 in) pieces
1 tablespoon olive oil
½ teaspoon Favourite Spice Mix (see page 34)

Preheat oven to 180°C (350°F). Place ingredients in a plastic bag and seal. Shake to coat the pumpkin with the oil and Favourite Spice Mix. Tip out onto an oven tray lined with baking paper. Bake until soft and golden brown in colour. Test with a skewer.

Asian-inspired roasted pumpkin

¼ Jap pumpkin, peeled and cut into 3 cm (1 in) pieces
1 tablespoon olive oil
1 tablespoon tamari
½ teaspoon Chinese five spice

Preheat oven to 180°C (350°F). Place all ingredients in a plastic bag and seal. Shake to coat the pumpkin with the oil, tamari and Chinese five spice. Tip out onto an oven tray lined with baking paper. Bake until soft and golden brown in colour. Test with a skewer.

NOTE: You can leave the skin on or off the pumpkin, depending on your preference.

Opposite page:
Preparing pumpkin for roasting

Yoghurt cheese balls

Yoghurt cheese is delicious marinated with lemon-flavoured oil and served with a salad or on top of steamed vegetables. It can also be used in lunch wraps instead of mayonnaise.

1 piece of muslin 30 cm (12 in) square

500 g (1.1 lb) Greek yoghurt

1 teaspoon Celtic sea salt

cooking string

1 teaspoon cracked black pepper

3 sprigs thyme

1 bay leaf

1 slice fresh lemon cut into 4

½ cup olive oil

½ cup lemon-flavoured olive oil

sterilised jar (see page 28 for instructions).

Sterilise the muslin by steeping it in boiling water. Drain and lay over a large plate. Mix the yoghurt with the salt and tip it on the muslin. Bring up the sides of the muslin and tie firmly with the string. Tie the muslin over a wooden spoon and rest the spoon over a saucepan so that the muslin bag is suspended. The saucepan will catch the whey as it drips off. If the weather is warm, place the saucepan in the refrigerator. Leave for 2 to 3 days until the yoghurt stops dripping. After three days the whey will be in the saucepan and a soft cheese will be in the muslin.

Store the whey in a jar in the refrigerator. Take teaspoons of the cheese and roll into balls with your hands. Lower gently into the sterilised jar and sprinkle with the cracked pepper. Place the thyme, bay leaf and lemon slices in the jar. Mix the two oils together and pour into the jar until the cheese is covered. Seal with the lid and store in the refrigerator. Allow 2 days for the Yoghurt Cheese Balls to marinate before using them. They will keep for up to two weeks in the refrigerator.

NOTE: Don't throw the whey out. Whey is a good source of minerals and digestive bacteria. It can be added to soups and stews to aid digestion. When used in marinades, it softens meat. You can also use it when baking bread.

Ratatouille

Ratatouille is really versatile and can be served hot or cold. It is really easy to make and can be stored for several days in the refrigerator.

4 serves

1 teaspoon olive oil
1 small Spanish onion, finely chopped
2 garlic cloves, finely chopped
1 red capsicum (pepper), cut into 1 cm ($\frac{1}{2}$ in) dice
1 green capsicum (pepper), cut into 1 cm ($\frac{1}{2}$ in) dice
2 large ripe tomatoes, cut into 1 cm ($\frac{1}{2}$ in) dice
1 small oriental eggplant (aubergine), cut into 1 cm ($\frac{1}{2}$ in) dice
1 small zucchini (courgette), cut into 1 cm ($\frac{1}{2}$ in) dice
pinch of Celtic sea salt
$\frac{1}{2}$ teaspoon Favourite Spice Mix (see page 34) or thyme sprig
1 teaspoon tomato paste
2 tablespoons white wine
sprig of thyme or a Rosemary Flavour Bag (see page 34)

Place a deep-sided frying pan or wok over medium heat. Add oil and sauté the onions and garlic for 2 minutes. Add the capsicum (pepper) and cook for another 2 minutes. Add tomatoes, eggplant (aubergine), zucchini (courgette), Celtic salt, spice mix, tomato paste, wine and flavour bag or thyme sprig. Reduce heat and cook gently for 15 minutes. Remove flavour bag or thyme sprig.

NOTE: Ratatouille can be served on French toast, with frittata, grilled fish, chicken or lamb. Other recipes in this book that include Ratatouille are Pan-seared Greek Cheese and Ratatouille Cottage Pie on page 88 and page 92.

Four easy salads

These salads are easy to make and can be added to any meal.

Fresh and crisp salad

1 serve

- 1 handful of mixed salad leaves, washed and dried
- 4 mint leaves, thinly sliced (preferably Vietnamese mint)
- 6 thin slices cucumber, cut on the diagonal
- 6 thin slices celery, cut on the diagonal
- 1 tablespoon Mustard and Orange Salad Dressing (see page 38)

Place all salad ingredients in a small bowl and toss together with the salad dressing. Serve immediately.

Pear and walnut salad

1 serve

- ½ a pear, cored and sliced
- 1 handful of mixed watercress and rocket leaves (arugula), washed and dried
- 1 tablespoon walnuts, roughly chopped
- half an orange, for squeezing
- olive oil, to drizzle
- pinch of Celtic sea salt
- cracked black pepper
- 1 tablespoon parmesan shavings

Place pear slices, watercress, rocket leaves and walnuts in a bowl. Squeeze orange juice on top and toss to mix. Drizzle with olive oil and season with Celtic salt and pepper. Serve immediately topped with the shaved parmesan.

Roasted beetroot (beet) salad

1 serve

- 1 handful of baby spinach leaves, washed and dried
- ½ roasted beetroot (beet), diced into 3 cm (1 in) cubes
- 1 tablespoon marinated goat's feta or 1 Yoghurt Cheese Ball (see page 44)
- 1 tablespoon pistachios or chopped walnuts
- ½ orange, for squeezing
- pinch of Celtic sea salt
- cracked black pepper

Mix together all ingredients in a small bowl and season with Celtic salt and pepper. Squeeze orange over salad. Serve immediately.

Tuscan salad

1 serve

- 4 cherry tomatoes, cut in half
- 4 bocconcini
- 6 basil leaves, torn
- 1 tablespoon baby olives (or 6 kalamata)
- olive oil, to drizzle

Mix all ingredients in a small bowl and drizzle with the olive oil. Serve immediately.

Overleaf, clockwise from top:
Roasted beetroot (beet) salad, Tuscan salad,
Fresh and crisp salad, Pear and walnut salad

Homemade yoghurt

The value in making your own yoghurt is that you can choose good quality organic milk. You will require a milk thermometer. It is important to use a sterilised jar (see page 28 for instructions).

1 litre (2 pints) organic milk
100 g (3.5 oz) biodynamic yoghurt

Place milk in a heavy based saucepan on the stove and heat to 80°C (175°F). Take off the heat and allow to cool to 50°C (120°F). Add the yoghurt and stir to combine. It's normal for the mixture to be a little bit lumpy.

Transfer to a sterilised, 1-litre (2-pint) jar. Put the lid on. Place the jar in a pan and fill the pan to the rim of the jar with hot water from the tap. The warmth will help to curdle the yoghurt. Leave in a warm part of your kitchen for 10 to 18 hours or until it thickens. Transfer to the refrigerator. The yoghurt will keep in the refrigerator for a few days.

NOTE: An electric yoghurt maker will make a smoother, thicker yoghurt. These can be purchased from department or electrical stores.

Preserved lemons

5 small lemons
¼ cup Celtic sea salt
1 tablespoon black peppercorns
2 bay leaves or a sprig of thyme
½ cup lemon juice
sterilised glass jar (see page 28 for instructions).
olive oil to cover

Cut lemons into quarters. Sprinkle salt over lemons and pack into a sterilised glass jar while layering with the peppercorns and fresh herbs. Press down firmly to squeeze out the juice. Add any remaining salt and the lemon juice.

Seal with the lid and store at room temperature in a cupboard. Turn the jar each day to redistribute the salt and lemon juice. After 7 days, open the jar and top up with olive oil. After 4 weeks the lemons will be softened and ready for use. They will keep for about 6 months.

NOTE: Preserved lemons are excellent rubbed onto the skin of a chicken before roasting or used in the stuffing. Use them to add flavour to Moroccan dishes, marinades, quinoa salads and casseroles or fish dishes.

Opposite page:
Preserved lemons

Basic roast chicken

Roasting a chicken every week is a great kitchen helper. There are so many quick meals that can be made from roasted chicken like chicken salads, chicken and salad wraps and fillings for rice paper rolls.

1 x size 12 free-range or organic chicken
4 pieces Preserved Lemon (see page 50)
1 onion, peeled and cut into quarters
1 oven bag for baking

Preheat oven to 180°C (350°F). Pat the chicken dry with a paper towel. Rub a preserved lemon quarter over the skin of the chicken and then place all the lemon pieces inside the cavity along with onion. Place chicken in the oven bag and onto a baking tray. Tie the top of the bag and make a couple of holes for the stream to escape.

Bake for 1 hour or until the chicken is cooked. Once chicken is cool, peel the skin off and discard. Leave some large pieces such as the drumsticks and shred the remaining chicken into pieces. Store in an airtight container in the refrigerator for use in other meals.

Green vegetable medley

On shopping day, I like to prepare my favourite vegetables and place them in individual parcels in zip-lock bags. They are easy to steam when you come home from a busy day. Simply flavour with a squeeze of lemon or orange juice, Celtic sea salt and cracked black pepper. Try with a Yoghurt Cheese Ball on top (see page 44) or a small piece of marinated goat's feta. Sprinkle over 2 finely chopped walnut halves or simply sprinkle with chopped parsley or coriander (cilantro).

1 serve

4 pieces broccolini (baby broccoli)
12 green beans
6 slices zucchini (courgette)
6 sugar snap peas
2 small bok choy

Lightly steam the vegetables for 2 to 3 minutes and add your favourite topping.

Homemade tomato sauce

Can be used to flavour soups or stews instead of tinned tomatoes.

    1 kilo (2.2 lb) very ripe tomatoes (Roma preferably)
    1 tablespoon olive oil
    1 large brown onion, roughly chopped
    2 large garlic cloves, roughly chopped
    ½ cup dry white wine
    1 tablespoon tomato paste
    1 heaped teaspoon Favourite Spice Mix (see page 34)
    1 teaspoon Sweet Chilli Sauce (see page 38)
    1 Rosemary Flavour Bag (see page 34)
    2 cups water
    ½ teaspoon Celtic sea salt
    cracked black pepper

Place a large saucepan of water on the stove and bring to the boil. Drop the tomatoes into the water a few at a time to blanch the skins. This only takes a couple of minutes. Remove with a slotted spoon, peel the skin off and cut out the core.

In another large pan, heat the olive oil and sauté the onions and garlic for 1 minute, being careful not to brown them. Add the wine, tomato paste, spice mix, chilli sauce, flavour bag, water and tomatoes. Season with Celtic salt and cracked pepper.

Bring to a simmer and cook uncovered for 40 minutes. Set aside to cool. Remove flavour bag and blend the tomato mixture in batches in a food processor or blender. Blend for a few seconds for a more chunky sauce or longer if you prefer a smoother sauce.

NOTE: Roasted Garlic (see page 38) can be used for a richer flavour. Sauce can be stored in small plastic containers in the freezer.

Spelt bread

1½ cups wholemeal spelt flour

1½ cups white spelt flour

1 teaspoon Celtic sea salt

1 teaspoon sugar

1 tablespoon dried yeast

2 teaspoons bread improver (optional)

¼ cup linseeds

2 tablespoons sesame seeds

1 tablespoon oil

1½ cups lukewarm water, plus an extra splash

Place spelt flours, Celtic salt, sugar, dried yeast, bread improver, linseeds and sesame seeds in a large bowl and mix together thoroughly. Drizzle the oil into the bowl and add the lukewarm water. Mix together to form a soft dough. (You may need to adjust the amount of water to reach this consistency.)

Lightly flour your work surface and knead the dough for about 5 minutes or until smooth and elastic. Place the dough back in the bowl and cover with a clean tea towel dampened with hot water. Place in a warm, draught-free spot until the bread dough doubles in size. This is called proving the dough and will take about 1¼ to 2 hours. Punch the dough down to remove the air and turn out onto the floured work surface. Knead again for about 5 minutes. Shape the dough into a loaf.

Place the dough in a greased and floured bread tin, cover again with the dampened tea towel and set aside to prove for another hour or until the dough doubles in size.

Preheat your oven to 200°C (400°F). Bake for about 25 to 30 minutes or until golden brown. Your sense of smell will tell you when your homemade bread is ready.

NOTE: Bread improver can help you make a great loaf of bread. Look for one made from non-genetically modified soy flour, ascorbic acid and amylase enzyme. A car sitting in the sun is a great incubator to prove your bread.

Homemade muesli

Homemade muesli is very nourishing and makes for a handy breakfast. It provides protein, essential fatty acids and fibre to give your digestive system a good workout. It also gives you energy from carbohydrates.

Makes 5½ cups

3 cups rolled oats
¼ cup linseeds
¼ cup sesame seeds
¼ cup sunflower seeds
¼ cup pepita seeds
½ cup currants
½ cup of almonds, roughly chopped or left whole
½ cup Brazil nuts, roughly chopped or left whole
12 pitted prunes, roughly chopped

In a large bowl mix all the ingredients together with a large spoon or with your hands. Place in a large glass jar with a good-fitting lid.

NOTE: You can use this as a base for bircher muesli or enjoy on its own with poached fruit.

Cooked quinoa

Quinoa is a high-protein grain and can be cooked in the same way as rice. I often make a double batch because quinoa is a great base for a salad.

My favourite way to cook quinoa is in a rice cooker. For a single serve, place ¼ cup of quinoa and ½ cup of water in a rice cooker and cook until ready.

If you do not have a rice cooker, place a medium-sized saucepan of water over high heat and bring to the boil. Add quinoa and reduce heat to a simmer. Cook for 10 minutes or until grains are just tender. Remove from heat and drain well.

Opposite page:
Homemade muesli

First up

You have been fasting throughout the night so a cleansing drink will help clear out the toxins and rehydrate your digestive system. Enzymes from raw food ingredients will kickstart your metabolism.

- Hot lemon drink with manuka honey
- Morning metabolism booster

Hot lemon drink with manuka honey

1 drink

Lemons are packed with vitamin C and provide an alkaline balance while cleansing the digestive system. They also act as a powerful solvent, reducing acid deposits in the joints and reducing uric acid in conditions such as gout, rheumatism and gallstones.

Lemon squeezed into hot water is a simple way to detoxify your body and a great way to kickstart your metabolism at the beginning of the day. Manuka honey is one of the finest quality honeys and has natural antibiotic properties.

½ lemon, squeezed
1 cup hot water
½ teaspoon manuka honey (optional)

Boil the kettle. Place lemon juice in your favourite cup with the honey. Pour the hot water into the cup and briskly stir. Sip slowly as it cools.

Morning metabolism booster

Fill your body with live enzymes and wake up your metabolism with fresh vegetables.

1 juice

1 stick celery
1 carrot
¼ small beetroot (beet)
small slice of ginger
1 green apple, cut into quarters
3 kale leaves (Tuscan cabbage)

Juice all ingredients in a juice extractor and drink immediately. The enzymes begin to oxidise as soon as you juice, so it doesn't store well.

Celery reduces acidity and relieves fluid retention. Its alkalising effect lessens a sweet tooth.

Carrot cleanses the liver and boosts the immune system. It also reduces inflammation in the intestines and has an insulin-like compound, which assists diabetics.

Beetroot (beet) aids digestion. It cleanses the blood, the lymphatic system and the liver. It also assists with iron deficiency.

Ginger has anti-inflammatory compounds reducing the effects of arthritis. It relieves stress in the digestive system and boosts the immune system to help fight infection.

Green apples stimulate the digestive system to cleanse itself by eliminating toxins from the small intestine. They are high in soluble fibre and improve the friendly bacteria in the digestive tract.

Kale (Tuscan cabbage) has a huge range of vitamins, minerals and antioxidants. It has an ingredient that causes the liver to produce enzymes that increase detoxification. When your liver is healthy, you feel energised.

I recommend the **Kuvings Silent Juicer**. This juicer gently presses the fruits and vegetables rather than high speed grinding and this keeps the enzymes intact and alive.

What I like the most is that it is quiet, so if you are up early to wake-up your metabolic clock you won't be waking up your family.

Go to **www.kuvings.net.au** for more information.

Breakfast

Eating breakfast cranks up the digestive furnace and gets your metabolism moving. An early breakfast will provide fuel for the day's activities.

- Poached peaches with homemade muesli and yoghurt
- Porridge with poached prunes
- Special occasion breakfast hotcakes with strawberries
- Asparagus and poached eggs
- Poached eggs with avocado
- Lemon ricotta bake with mushrooms and spinach
- French toast with roasted Roma tomatoes
- French toast with avocado salsa

Poached peaches with homemade muesli and yoghurt

Other stone fruits that can be poached include apricots and nectarines.

2 meals

4 peaches
1 cup organic apple juice
1 cup water
seeds of ½ vanilla bean
1 cinnamon stick
4 tablespoons Homemade Muesli (see page 56)
4 tablespoons natural yoghurt or use Homemade Yoghurt
  (see page 50)

Place a small saucepan over medium heat. Add whole peaches, apple juice, water, seeds of vanilla bean and cinnamon stick and bring to the boil. Reduce heat to low. Simmer for 10 to 15 minutes or until peaches are tender.

Test peaches with a skewer. Remove peaches and cinnamon stick with a slotted spoon and set aside. Increase the heat and reduce the syrup by half.

Divide peaches and cooking juice between 2 bowls and add 2 tablespoons muesli and 2 tablespoons yoghurt to each bowl.

Porridge with poached prunes

2 meals

1 cup organic apple juice
10 pitted prunes
2 teaspoons manuka honey
1 cinnamon stick
1 cup rolled oats
2 cups water, for soaking
2 cups water, extra
pinch of Celtic sea salt
½ cup milk, (optional)

Place a small saucepan over medium heat and add the apple juice, prunes, honey and cinnamon stick. Simmer until the sauce reduces to a sticky consistency. Cool overnight. Before going to bed, place rolled oats in soaking water in a small saucepan and leave to soak overnight.

Next morning, drain the water off the oats and add the extra water. Place the saucepan over medium heat, stir frequently with a wooden spoon and bring to the boil. Reduce heat and continue to cook for another 3 to 4 minutes or until oats are soft and creamy. Stir in salt. Pour the milk into the oats and mix through. Spoon into 2 bowls and top with the prunes and sticky juices. Serve immediately.

NOTE: If you have allergies to cow's milk you can substitute with soy or rice milk or any other milk alternative that you normally use.

Special occasion breakfast hotcakes with strawberries

2 meals

1 free-range or organic egg, separated
pinch of Celtic sea salt
¼ cup ricotta cheese
¾ cup buttermilk
¼ teaspoon vanilla essence
½ cup white spelt flour
¼ teaspoon baking powder
25 g (1 oz) butter
100 g (3.5 oz) strawberries, sliced
2 tablespoons manuka honey or pure maple syrup
2 lemon wedges to squeeze

Place the egg white in a bowl with a pinch of Celtic salt and whisk until soft white peaks form. Place the ricotta, buttermilk, vanilla essence and egg yolk in a medium-sized bowl and mix together with a hand or electric beater. Sift together the spelt flour and baking powder. Add to the ricotta mixture and mix well. Gently fold in the egg white with a spatula.

Heat a non-stick frying pan and melt half the butter. To make breakfast hotcakes, drop tablespoons of batter into the hot pan. Make three hotcakes at a time. Cook over a medium heat for two minutes and turn over with a spatula. Cook until golden on both sides. Wipe pan with a paper towel and melt the remaining butter and cook another batch.

To serve, pile 3 hotcakes onto a plate and top with sliced strawberries. Drizzle honey or maple syrup over the top. Serve with the lemon wedges.

Asparagus and poached eggs

1 meal

2 free-range or organic eggs
1 tablespoon white vinegar
1 slice spelt or multigrain bread
5 pieces asparagus, ends trimmed
½ lemon for squeezing
handful of rocket (arugula) or
    watercress leaves, washed and dried
1 tablespoon shaved parmesan cheese
pinch of Celtic sea salt
cracked black pepper

Place a saucepan with a steamer over medium heat and half fill with boiling water. This is to cook the asparagus while your eggs are poaching.

Break the eggs into a cup to ensure the yolks are intact. Fill a deep-sided saucepan with at least 10 cm (4 in) of simmering water. Add the vinegar to the water. Stir the water with a spoon, creating a small whirlpool. Drop the eggs one at a time into the centre of the whirlpool. The water will settle and the eggs should form an oval.

While the eggs are cooking, chargrill or toast the bread. Place the asparagus in the steamer for 90 seconds. Remove pan from heat and squeeze lemon juice on top of asparagus.

Place toast on a plate and arrange the watercress or rocket (arugula) leaves and asparagus on top. Remove the eggs with a slotted spoon and drain well. Place the eggs on the toast and asparagus, sprinkle with the parmesan shavings and season with Celtic salt and cracked black pepper.

Poached eggs with avocado

1 meal

2 free-range or organic eggs
1 tablespoon white vinegar
1 slice spelt or multigrain bread
½ avocado, sliced
½ lemon, for squeezing
Celtic sea salt
cracked black pepper

Break the eggs into a cup to ensure the yolk is intact. Fill a deep-sided saucepan with at least 10 cm (4 in) of simmering water. Add the vinegar to the water. Stir the water with a spoon, creating a small whirlpool. Slowly drop the eggs one at a time into the centre of the whirlpool. The water will settle and the eggs should form an oval. While the eggs are cooking chargrill or toast the bread.

Place the toast on a plate and arrange the avocado on top. Squeeze the lemon juice on the avocado. Remove the eggs with a slotted spoon and drain well. Place the eggs on the toast and season with Celtic salt and cracked black pepper.

Opposite page:
Asparagus and poached eggs

Lemon ricotta bake with mushrooms and spinach

2 meals

butter, for greasing

flour (spelt), for dusting

250 g (9 oz) fresh ricotta

1 tablespoon grated parmesan cheese

½ teaspoon finely grated lemon zest

pinch of cracked black pepper

pinch of Celtic sea salt

1 free-range or organic egg, separated

1 tablespoon oil

200 g (7 oz) assorted mushrooms such as oyster, shiitake, Swiss brown or shimeji

2 handfuls baby spinach leaves, washed and dried

2 slices spelt or multigrain bread

pinch of Celtic sea salt and cracked pepper

2 lemon wedges for squeezing

1 sprig flat-leaf parsley, leaves only

Preheat oven to 180°C (350°F). Grease and flour 2 x 200 ml (½ pint) ramekins.

Place ricotta, parmesan, lemon zest, cracked pepper, Celtic salt and egg yolk in a food processor and blend until smooth. Transfer to a larger bowl.

In a small bowl, beat the egg white until soft peaks form. Gently fold the egg white into the ricotta mixture. Divide into the ramekins. Smooth the top and bake for 20-25 minutes or until golden.

While the ricotta is baking, place a small frying pan over high heat and add the oil. Sauté the mushrooms for about six minutes or until just tender. Take pan off the heat and add the spinach leaves. Toss until the spinach leaves soften, then cover and keep warm. Toast the bread.

Gently turn the lemon ricotta bake out onto two plates. Season the mushroom and spinach with Celtic salt and pepper and arrange on the plate with the toasted bread. Serve with the lemon wedges and parsley.

NOTE: This can also be a midday meal.

French toast with roasted Roma tomatoes

1 meal

2 ripe Roma tomatoes
olive oil for drizzling
Celtic sea salt
Cracked black pepper
2 sprigs thyme
1 free-range or organic egg
2 tablespoons milk, (optional)
1 teaspoon olive oil
1 slice spelt or multigrain bread
25 g (1 oz) goat's feta, crumbled
handful rocket (arugula) leaves, washed
  and dried

Preheat oven to 180°C (350°F).

Slice tomatoes in half lengthways. Place on a small baking tray. Drizzle with olive oil and season with Celtic salt and cracked black pepper. Break up the thyme and sprinkle over the tomatoes. Bake until tender.

In a small, flat bowl, whisk the egg, milk, Celtic salt and cracked pepper. Place a non-stick frying pan over medium heat and add olive oil to heat.

Dip the bread in the egg mixture until well covered. Add to the pan and cook on both sides until golden brown and slightly crisp. Place on a serving plate, top with roasted tomatoes, goat's feta and rocket (arugula). Serve immediately.

NOTE: This can also be a midday meal. Make a larger batch of Roasted Roma Tomatoes to add to salads or other meals. Other toppings for French toast include Ratatouille (see page 46) and Tomato Relish (see page 119).

French toast with avocado salsa

1 meal

½ avocado, chopped into 1 cm (½ in)
  cubes
25 g (1 oz) marinated goat's feta,
  crumbled
1 sprig coriander (cilantro) or flat-leaf
  parsley, leaves only
½ lemon for squeezing
1 free-range or organic egg
2 tablespoons milk (optional)
Celtic sea salt
Cracked pepper
1 teaspoon olive oil
1 slice spelt or multigrain bread
handful rocket (arugula) leaves, washed
  and dried

Combine the avocado, goat's feta, coriander (cilantro) or parsley, squeeze of lemon juice and cracked pepper in a bowl. Mix to combine. Set aside.

In a small, flat bowl, whisk the egg, milk, Celtic salt and cracked pepper. Place a non-stick frying pan over medium heat and add olive oil to heat. Dip the bread in egg mixture until well covered. Add to pan and cook on both sides until golden brown and slightly crisp. Place on serving plate, top with salsa mixture and rocket (arugula). Serve immediately.

NOTE: This can also be a midday meal.

Opposite page:
French toast with
avocado salsa

Mid-morning fruit

Eat fruit around 10 am – it is very easy and makes a portable snack.

Raw fruit is full of life-giving enzymes that will speed up your metabolism. The fibre and water content in the fruit will create the right variables for digestive vitality. Make sure you include lots of variety for the antioxidants and trace minerals.

If you are hungry after eating fruit mid-morning, this means that your metabolism is speeding up and you can look forward to enjoying your midday meal. Pineapple contains an enzyme called bromelain, which burns fat, so this is a particularly good fruit to eat at this time. Choose from the following:

- 2 slices fresh pineapple
- 5 cherries and a peach
- 1 pear and 1 kiwifruit
- 2 kiwifruit
- 1 peach and 1 passionfruit
- 1 pear and 1 apple
- 2 mandarins
- small bunch grapes
- 2 apricots
- 1 nectarine and a peach
- 1 peach and 6 raspberries
- 4 strawberries, 8 blueberries and 8 raspberries

Opposite page:
A selection of fresh fruit

Midday meal

Eat a nourishing meal close to midday when your metabolism is most active. This will provide you with the fuel for an energetic afternoon.

- Olive and onion spelt pizza
- Zucchini (courgette) and goat's feta spelt pizza
- Pumpkin and spinach frittata with pear and walnut salad
- Eggplant (aubergine) and egg salad
- Tuscan bean and spinach soup
- Vegetable fritters with minted yoghurt dip
- Lentil soup
- Baked giant beans, three ways
- Pan-seared Greek cheese, two ways
- Spinach and ricotta gnocchi, two ways
- Ratatouille cottage pie
- Vegetarian rice paper rolls
- Chicken and avocado rice paper rolls
- Simple seafood soup
- Ricotta and tuna lunch slice with roasted capsicums (peppers)
- Easy chicken lunch wrap
- Chicken, avocado and mango salad
- Asian chicken salad

Olive and onion spelt pizza

2 meals

2 tablespoons olive oil

2 medium brown onions, sliced thinly into rings

2 sprigs fresh thyme

cracked pepper

½ cup of spelt flour, white or wholemeal

50 g (1.75 oz) butter, diced

1 tablespoon grated parmesan cheese

¼ teaspoon Celtic sea salt

2 tablespoons cold water

¼ cup sun-dried tomatoes

8 kalamata olives, pitted and halved

extra teaspoon parmesan cheese

Preheat the oven to 180°C (350°F).

Heat the oil in a large non-stick frying pan over medium heat. Add the onions to the pan. Rub the thyme in your hands to break up the leaves and add to the pan. Sauté for 20 minutes, stirring occasionally. The onions will turn golden brown. Season with cracked pepper and set aside to cool.

To make the pizza base, place the spelt flour, butter, parmesan cheese and Celtic salt in a food processor and mix for a few seconds. Add the cold water and mix to form a soft dough. You may need to adjust the amount of water. Roll onto a lightly floured surface and knead for a few minutes. Wrap in plastic and place in the refrigerator for 20 minutes.

Place the pizza base onto a lightly floured surface and with a rolling pin, form a 15 x 30 cm (6 x 12 in) roughly shaped rectangle. Place on a tray lined with baking paper.

Place sun-dried tomatoes in a food processor and blend to a smooth paste. Spread the pizza base with the sun-dried tomato paste and top with the onion mixture and olives. Sprinkle with the extra parmesan cheese. Bake for 20 to 25 minutes or until pizza is cooked. Serve warm with a salad.

NOTE: You can purchase a jar of sun-dried tomatoes, drain off the oil and blend into a paste. Return to jar, seal and store in the refrigerator.

Zucchini (courgette) and goat's feta spelt pizza

2 meals

½ cup of spelt flour, white or wholemeal

50 g (1.75 oz) butter, diced

1 tablespoon grated parmesan cheese

¼ teaspoon Celtic sea salt

2 tablespoons cold water

1 medium zucchini (courgette), sliced into thin ribbons – use a mandolin if you have one

¼ cup sun-dried tomatoes

50 g (1.75 oz) goat's feta, crumbled

2 sprigs fresh thyme

cracked pepper

extra teaspoon parmesan cheese

Preheat the oven to 180°C (350°F).

To make the pizza base, place the spelt flour, butter, parmesan cheese and Celtic salt in a food processor and mix for a few seconds. Add the cold water and mix to form a soft dough. You may need to adjust the amount of water. Roll onto a lightly floured surface and knead for a few minutes. Wrap in plastic and place in the refrigerator for 20 minutes.

Place the pizza base onto a lightly floured surface and with a rolling pin form a 15 x 30 cm (6 x 12 in) roughly shaped rectangle. Place on a tray lined with baking paper.

Place sun-dried tomatoes in a food processor and blend to a smooth paste. Spread the pastry with the sun-dried tomato paste and top with the zucchini (courgette) ribbons and crumbled goat's feta. Rub the thyme in your hands to break up the leaves over the pizza. Sprinkle with cracked pepper and the extra parmesan cheese. Bake for 20 to 25 minutes or until pizza is cooked. Serve warm with a salad.

Left: Olive and onion spelt pizza
Right: Zucchini (courgette) and goat's feta spelt pizza

Pumpkin and spinach frittata with pear and walnut salad

2 meals

250 g (9 oz) peeled Jap pumpkin, cut into 2 cm (¾ in) cubes

2 teaspoons olive oil, plus extra for brushing

½ teaspoon Favourite Spice Mix (see page 34)

½ cup sliced leek, white part only

2 garlic cloves, finely chopped

100 g (3.5 oz) baby spinach leaves, washed and dried

3 free-range or organic eggs

1 tablespoon natural yoghurt

Celtic salt and cracked black pepper

50 g (1.75 oz) feta cheese, crumbled

2 tablespoons grated parmesan cheese

2 serves of Pear and Walnut Salad (see page 47)

Preheat oven to 180°C (350°F).

Place pumpkin, 1 teaspoon of olive oil and spice mix in a small plastic bag and seal. Shake to coat the pumpkin with the oil and spice mix. Tip out onto an oven tray lined with baking paper. Bake for approximately 15 minutes or until soft and golden brown in colour. Test with a skewer.

Place a non-stick frying pan over medium heat. Add remaining 1 teaspoon of olive oil and cook leek for 2 minutes, then add the garlic and cook for another minute. Remove from heat and stir through the spinach leaves so that they wilt. Set aside to cool.

Brush a square casserole dish or small baking tin with olive oil. In a medium bowl, whisk together eggs, yoghurt a pinch of Celtic salt and cracked pepper. Roughly chop the leek and spinach mixture and gently stir into the egg mixture. Add the cooked pumpkin and crumbled feta cheese and stir gently to mix.

Pour into the prepared dish or pan and top with parmesan cheese. Place in preheated oven and bake for 25 minutes or until golden and set. Serve with Pear and Walnut Salad.

Eggplant (aubergine) and egg salad

2 meals

2 oriental eggplants (aubergines)
½ butter lettuce, leaves washed and dried
2 spring onions, sliced thinly
2 free-range or organic eggs, hard-boiled and cut into wedges
½ small Lebanese cucumber, sliced
6 cherry tomatoes cut in half
1 tablespoon roughly chopped walnuts
1 sprig coriander (cilantro), leaves

For the dressing

½ teaspoon fish sauce
2 tablespoons lime juice
1 teaspoon Sweet Chilli Sauce (see page 38)
2 tablespoons olive oil

Preheat the oven to 180°C (350°F).

Place the eggplant (aubergine) on a baking tray and place in the oven. Cook until tender. Transfer to a bowl, cover with cling wrap and leave for 5 minutes. This will soften the skin. Chop the eggplants (aubergine), into cubes.

In 2 bowls arrange the butter lettuce leaves, eggplant (aubergine), spring onions, hard-boiled eggs, cucumber slices and cherry tomatoes. Make the dressing by mixing together the ingredients in a jar with a tight-fitting lid. Drizzle dressing over salad and top with chopped walnuts and coriander (cilantro) leaves.

NOTE: Oriental eggplants (aubergines) are long and thin.

Tuscan bean and spinach soup

2 meals

1 cup fresh borlotti beans

2 tablespoons olive oil

$\frac{1}{2}$ small leek, white part only, finely chopped

2 garlic cloves, finely chopped

$\frac{1}{2}$ cup dry white wine

1 Rosemary Flavour Bag (see page 34)

1 teaspoon tomato paste

2 cups vegetable stock

1 sprig flat-leaf parsley, chopped

2 handfuls English spinach leaves, washed, stalks removed and chopped

pinch of Celtic sea salt

cracked black pepper

2 slices spelt or wholegrain bread

Heat 1 litre (2 pints) of water in a pot. Add the beans and simmer for 40 minutes or until the beans are tender. Taste a bean to test.

In the meantime, heat the olive oil in a deep-sided saucepan and sauté the leeks for 1 minute. Add the garlic and cook for 1 minute. Then add the wine, flavour bag, tomato paste and vegetable stock. Bring to the boil then reduce to a simmer for 45 minutes.

Drain the cooked beans, saving half a cup of the liquid. Set aside half the beans. Put the remaining beans and saved liquid in a food processor and pulse for 10 seconds to roughly chop. Or, if you have a stick blender, return the beans and the half cup of cooking water to the pot and pulse for a few seconds to form a paste.

Add the pulsed beans to the soup mix with the parsley, the beans that were set aside and the spinach leaves and cook gently for a few minutes. Season to taste with Celtic salt and cracked black pepper and serve immediately with bread.

NOTE: If fresh borlotti beans are not available use 1 cup of dried borlotti beans. Soak them in water the night before. When cooking the beans, do not add salt because this toughens the skins. They will take a little longer than fresh beans.

Vegetable fritters with minted yoghurt dip

2 meals

250 g (9 oz) zucchini (courgette), grated
½ cup rice flour
1 sprig fresh coriander (cilantro), chopped
1 tablespoon grated parmesan cheese
1 small free-range or organic egg, lightly beaten
½ teaspoon finely grated lemon zest
Celtic sea salt and cracked black pepper
1 tablespoon olive oil
1 quantity Minted Yoghurt Dip (see below)
handful of rocket (arugula) leaves, washed and dried

Squeeze the grated zucchini (courgette) dry in a tea towel or muslin and place in a medium-sized bowl. It's really important to squeeze out as much water as possible from the zucchini (courgette) to ensure that the fritters are crisp when cooked.

Add the rice flour, coriander (cilantro), parmesan cheese, egg, lemon zest, salt and pepper to the bowl and using your hands, mix. Divide the mixture into six evenly sized balls and flatten slightly into patties. Dust with rice flour. Chill in the refrigerator for 15 minutes.

Heat olive oil in a large non-stick frying pan. Add the patties and cook for 3 minutes on each side or until golden and cooked through. Serve with Minted Yoghurt Dip and rocket (arugula) leaves.

NOTE: Vegetable Fritters can also be served with Ratatouille (see page 46), Roasted Pumpkin (see page 42) or Tomato Relish (see page 119).

Minted yoghurt dip

1 cup natural yoghurt
8 small mint leaves, finely chopped
8 cm (3 in) length cucumber, grated

Gently combine all ingredients and place in a small bowl.

Lentil soup

4 meals

1 tablespoon olive oil
1 small onion, finely chopped
2 garlic cloves, peeled and finely chopped
1 celery stalk, finely chopped
8 cm (3 inch) piece of sweet potato, peeled and finely chopped
1 small potato, peeled and finely chopped
1 small carrot, peeled and finely chopped
¼ cup dry white wine
250 g (9 oz) red lentils
400 g (14 oz) tin diced tomatoes
2 cups vegetable stock
2 cups water
½ teaspoon tomato paste
1 teaspoon Favourite Spice Mix (see page 34)
cracked black pepper
1 sprig flat-leaf parsley, finely chopped
4 slices spelt or wholegrain bread

Heat oil in a large saucepan over medium heat. Cook onion for
1 minute then add garlic for another minute. Add celery, sweet
potato, potato and carrot and stir for 2 minutes. Add wine, stirring
for 40 seconds. Add lentils, diced tomatoes, stock, water, tomato
paste, spice mix and pepper. Cover and bring to the boil, then reduce
heat and simmer covered for about 1 hour or until the potatoes
and carrots are tender. Remove from the heat and stir through the
parsley. Ladle into four bowls and serve with bread.

NOTE: For a non-vegetarian version, add a smoked bacon bone when
cooking the soup to add more flavour.

Baked giant beans, three ways

4 meals

1 cup dried butter (lima) beans

1 tablespoon olive oil

8 cm (3 in) piece leek, finely diced

1 small stick celery, finely diced

1 carrot, finely diced

2 garlic cloves, finely chopped

1 tablespoon fresh oregano or 1 teaspoon dried

¼ cup dry white wine

1 x 400 g (14 oz) tin diced tomatoes or 1 ½ cups Homemade
Tomato Sauce (see page 53)

1 teaspoon tomato paste diluted in 1 cup of hot water

½ teaspoon cumin

½ teaspoon hot paprika

1 tablespoon flat-leaf parsley, finely chopped

Celtic sea salt and cracked pepper

Soak beans in a large bowl with plenty of water. Leave overnight.

The next day, drain the beans, wash and drain again. Tip the beans
into a large pot and cover with water. Bring to the boil. Cook for
30 minutes or until tender. Check often to avoid overcooking. Do
not add salt because this can toughen the skin of the beans. Drain
the cooked beans. Discard any loose skins.

Preheat the oven to 180°C (350°F).

Heat the olive oil in a large pan and cook the leek for 2 minutes. Add
the celery, carrot, garlic and oregano and stir with a wooden spoon
for 2 minutes. Add the wine, tomatoes or Homemade Tomato Sauce,
tomato paste and spices. Cook for 5 minutes. Add the cooked beans,
parsley and season with Celtic salt and cracked pepper.

Tip the bean mixture into a lightly oiled baking dish and bake for
30 to 35 minutes uncovered. Taste the beans to see if they are soft.
If the beans start to dry out, add a little water.

Serve with French Toast, a Fresh and Crisp Salad or Grilled Chicken.

NOTE: See over the page for serving instructions.

Baked giant beans serving instructions

Served with French toast

1 meal

Follow the instructions for French Toast (see page 70) and top with
¾ cup of Baked Giant Beans. Garnish with a little chopped parsley –
the enzymes will help your body digest the cooked food.

Served with a fresh and crisp salad

1 meal

Serve ¾ cup of Baked giant beans with a Fresh and Crisp salad.
(see page 47).

Served with grilled chicken

1 meal

1 organic chicken breast 200 g (7 oz)
1 teaspoon olive oil
pinch of Celtic sea salt
cracked pepper
¾ cup Baked Giant Beans
1 teaspoon flat-leaf parsley, finely chopped

Heat a frying pan on the stove. Brush the chicken with oil and season
with Celtic salt and pepper. Place in the pan and cook until tender.
Place the warm Baked Giant Beans in the centre of a plate and place
chicken on top. Garnish with parsley.

Opposite page:
Baked giant beans served
with a fresh and crisp salad

Pan-seared Greek cheese, two ways

Kefalograviera or saganaki is a Greek sheep's milk cheese available from gourmet food stores. If unavailable, substitute with haloumi cheese. Sumac is a Middle-Eastern spice that adds great flavour to the cheese.

1 serve

1 tablespoon white spelt flour

1 slice, approximately 150 g (5.25 oz) Greek sheep's milk cheese or haloumi

1 tablespoon olive oil

pinch of sumac

1 lemon wedge, for squeezing

Tip the flour onto a chopping board. Coat the cheese in the flour. Heat olive oil in a frying pan and cook the cheese for 2 minutes each side. Serve immediately with a pinch of sumac, a lemon wedge and a Greek Salad or Ratatouille.

Served with a Greek salad

1 meal

4 baby cos (romaine) lettuce leaves, washed and dried

4 cherry tomatoes, sliced in half

¼ Spanish onion, thinly sliced

4 cucumber slices, cut on the diagonal

4 mint leaves, torn

1 sprig flat-leaf parsley, leaves only

6 kalamata olives, or 8 baby olives

olive oil, to drizzle

Arrange the salad on a plate and drizzle with olive oil. Place cooked cheese on top and serve immediately.

Served with ratatouille

1 meal

4 baby cos (romaine) lettuce leaves, washed and dried

1 cup Ratatouille (see page 46)

To serve, place Ratatouille in the centre of a plate. Arrange cooked cheese on top. Serve with lettuce leaves on the side.

Opposite page:
Pan-seared Greek cheese
served with a Greek salad

Spinach and ricotta gnocchi, two ways

2 meals

150 g (5 oz) spinach

3 sprigs flat-leaf parsley

150 g (5 oz) fresh ricotta cheese

1 small free-range or organic egg, beaten

8 basil leaves, thinly sliced

pinch of cracked black pepper

1 heaped teaspoon white spelt flour

2 tablespoons grated parmesan cheese

Bring a large pot of water to the boil. Add spinach and parsley for 30 seconds to wilt. With a pair of tongs, remove spinach and parsley and transfer to a sieve. Run under cold water for 30 seconds to halt the cooking process. While in the sieve, squeeze out the excess water. Place on a chopping board and finely chop.

Transfer to a bowl and add ricotta, egg, basil, pepper, flour and parmesan. Mix together thoroughly. Roll a heaped dessertspoon, approximately 30 g (1 oz) of ricotta mixture into a ball or oval shape. Repeat and place in a single layer on a flour-dusted tray. Place in refrigerator for 20 minutes. Serve in Vegetable Broth or with Homemade Tomato Sauce.

Served with homemade tomato sauce

2 meals

1 batch of Spinach and Ricotta Gnocchi

2 cups Homemade Tomato Sauce (see page 53)

2 tablespoons grated parmesan cheese

1 tablespoon flat-leaf parsley, finely chopped

2 serves Fresh and Crisp Salad (see page 47)

Preheat oven to 180°C (350°F).

Pour the tomato sauce into a small baking tray and gently add the gnocchi. Sprinkle parmesan cheese on top and bake for 30 minutes. Remove baking dish from oven and sprinkle with parsley. Serve with Fresh and Crisp Salad.

Served in vegetable broth

2 meals

1 batch of Spinach and Ricotta Gnocchi

3 cups of vegetable stock

12 baby spinach leaves for garnish

Bring stock to a simmer in a large saucepan. Add dumplings in two batches and cook until they rise to the surface (1 to 2 minutes). Remove with a slotted spoon and place in two serving bowls. Place 6 baby spinach leaves in each bowl and ladle over stock. Serve immediately.

Opposite page:
Spinach and ricotta gnocchi
with homemade tomato sauce

Ratatouille cottage pie

4 meals

Potatoes have a high GI so this is recommended as a lunchtime meal in order to burn off the energy during the day.

  2 large potatoes, peeled and coarsely chopped
  2 teaspoons of butter
  pinch of Celtic sea salt
  1 x 400 g (14 oz) tin red kidney beans, rinsed and drained
  1 quantity Ratatouille (see page 46)
  olive oil for greasing
  2 tablespoons grated parmesan cheese
  1 teaspoon sesame seeds
  4 serves Fresh and Crisp Salad (see page 47)

Fill a deep-sided saucepan with 10 cm (4 in) of simmering water. Add the chopped potatoes and cook until tender. Drain well and mash with the butter and mix until smooth. Season to taste with Celtic salt.

Preheat oven to 180°C (350°F).

Stir the kidney beans through the Ratatouille mixture and spoon the mixture into a lightly oiled, small baking dish. Spread the mashed potato on top and sprinkle with parmesan cheese and sesame seeds. Bake for 30 minutes or until the top browns slightly. Serve with Fresh and Crisp salad.

Vegetarian rice paper rolls

1 meal

2 rice paper wrappers

¼ cup shredded iceberg lettuce

small handful bean sprouts

½ small carrot, peeled and grated

½ small Lebanese cucumber, cut into ribbons

½ medium avocado, peeled and cut into strips

3 small mint leaves, torn

3 Vietnamese mint leaves, torn

Sweet Chilli Sauce (see page 38), to serve

Pour warm water into a large heat-proof bowl until half full. Dip 1 rice paper wrapper in water for 10 seconds. Place on a damp tea towel on a flat surface. Stand for 20 to 30 seconds or until soft enough to roll without splitting.

Place half the lettuce along 1 edge of 1 wrapper. Top with half of each of the bean sprouts, carrot, cucumber, avocado and mint. Fold in ends. Roll up firmly to enclose filling. Repeat with remaining wrapper. Serve with Sweet Chilli Sauce.

Chicken and avocado rice paper rolls

1 meal

2 rice paper wrappers

½ cup cooked chicken, shredded (see page 52)

½ avocado, sliced thinly

½ small Lebanese cucumber, cut into thin strips

5 Vietnamese mint leaves, torn

1 sprig coriander (cilantro), leaves only

Sweet Chilli Sauce (see page 38), for dipping

Pour warm water into a large heat-proof bowl until half full. Dip 1 rice paper wrapper in water for 10 seconds. Place on a damp tea towel on a flat surface. Stand for 20 to 30 seconds or until soft enough to roll without splitting.

Place half of the chicken along 1 edge of 1 wrapper. Top with half of each of the sliced avocado, cucumber, mint and coriander (cilantro). Fold in ends. Roll up firmly to enclose filling. Repeat with remaining wrapper. Serve with Sweet Chilli Sauce.

Opposite page:
Vegetarian rice paper rolls
and Chicken and avocado
rice paper rolls

Simple seafood soup

2 meals

1 tablespoon olive oil
1 small brown onion, finely chopped
2 garlic cloves, finely chopped
½ cup dry white wine
1 teaspoon tomato paste
½ teaspoon Favourite Spice Mix (see page 34)
¼ teaspoon fennel seeds
½ teaspoon Sweet Chilli Sauce (see page 38)
½ teaspoon finely chopped fresh chilli
½ teaspoon fish sauce
1 small potato, cut into 1 cm (½ in) cubes
½ x 400 g (14 oz) tin diced tomatoes
2½ cups hot water
400 g (14 oz) seafood marinara mix
1 teaspoon finely chopped flat-leaf parsley
Celtic sea salt and cracked black pepper
2 slices spelt or multigrain bread

Heat oil in a large saucepan and cook the onion for 1 minute then add the garlic and cook for 1 minute. Add the wine, tomato paste, spice mix, fennel seeds, Sweet Chilli Sauce, fresh chilli, fish sauce, potato, tomatoes and 2½ cups hot water. Simmer covered for 20 minutes or until the potato is cooked.

Add the marinara mix and cook for 5 minutes with the lid on. Stir in the parsley and season with Celtic salt and pepper. Ladle into two bowls and serve immediately with the bread.

NOTE: Freeze the other half of the tinned tomatoes.

Ricotta and tuna lunch slice with roasted capsicums (peppers)

6 meals

2 red capsicums (peppers)
1 teaspoon olive oil
1 small leek (white part only), finely chopped
2 handfuls of baby spinach leaves
500 g (1.1 lb) fresh ricotta cheese
2 eggs, separated
¼ cup Greek yoghurt
1 tablespoon chopped flat-leaf parsley
½ cup grated parmesan cheese
1 tablespoon white spelt flour
¼ teaspoon Celtic sea salt
cracked black pepper
185 g (6.5 oz) tin tuna, drained
mixed salad leaves, washed and dried
4 cherry tomatoes, halved
4 slices cucumber

Preheat oven to 180°C (350°F). Grease and line a 20–22 cm (8–9 in) round, springform tin.

Place whole capsicums (peppers) on an oven tray and bake for 1 hour. Remove capsicums (peppers) from oven, place in a bowl and cover with plastic. Set aside to cool. When cool, you will easily be able to peel off the skins and discard the seeds. Tear into long strips and store in an airtight container in the refrigerator.

Heat olive oil in a non-stick frying pan and sauté the leek for 2 minutes. Add spinach leaves and toss to wilt. Set aside to cool.

Place the ricotta, egg yolks and yoghurt in a food processor and mix until smooth. Transfer to a large bowl and stir in the cooked leek, spinach leaves and parsley.

Beat the egg whites in a separate bowl until soft peaks form. Using a rubber spatula, gently fold the egg whites into the ricotta mixture with half the parmesan cheese, spelt flour, Celtic salt, cracked pepper and tuna. Place in the prepared pan and top with the remaining parmesan cheese.

Bake for 40 minutes covered with a piece foil. This prevents the top from burning. Remove foil and bake for a further 10 minutes to brown the top. Cool for a couple of minutes in the tin before removing. Serve with salad leaves, cherry tomatoes, cucumber and baked capsicum (peppers).

NOTE: This is easy to take to work. Pack salad in a plastic container and Ricotta and Tuna Lunch Slice in a separate container so it is ready to reheat at work.

Easy chicken lunch wrap

1 meal

1 wrap (flat/pocket/Mexican bread)

1 teaspoon Lemon Mayonnaise (see page 38)

½ avocado

squeeze lemon juice

¼ cup roast chicken, shredded (see page 52)

handful mixed salad leaves, washed and dried

4 slices cucumber

handful of sprouts, (optional)

cracked black pepper

Place flat bread on a chopping board and spread with the mayonnaise. Spoon the avocado on top and mash, spreading over the bread. Squeeze the lemon juice over the avocado. Place the chicken on half the bread followed by the salad leaves, cucumber and sprouts, if using. Sprinkle with the cracked pepper. Roll up from the chicken side. Eat immediately or wrap in baking paper ready for your midday meal.

Chicken, avocado and mango salad

2 meals

1 cup roast chicken, loosely shredded (see page 52)

1 avocado, sliced

1 small mango, sliced

6 cherry tomatoes, cut in half

2 handfuls mixed salad leaves, washed and dried

8 slices Lebanese cucumber, sliced on the diagonal

1 spring onion, sliced on the diagonal

6 sugar snap peas, thinly sliced into matchsticks

6 Vietnamese mint leaves, torn (optional)

2 tablespoons Mustard and Orange Salad Dressing (see page 38)

Place all salad ingredients in a bowl and mix together. Pour salad dressing over and toss through. Divide between 2 bowls.

Asian chicken salad

2 meals

1 organic chicken breast 200 g (7oz)
1 teaspoon olive oil
pinch of Celtic sea salt
cracked black pepper
handful of bean sprouts
1 spring onion, finely sliced on the diagonal
1 cup Chinese cabbage, finely shredded
½ small carrot, cut into matchsticks
½ medium Lebanese cucumber, cut into matchsticks
handful of watercress or butter lettuce leaves, washed and dried
10 Vietnamese mint leaves, torn
2 pieces Preserved Lemon (see page 50), finely chopped or
   ½ teaspoon finely grated lemon zest
6 macadamia nuts (or walnuts), roughly chopped

For the dressing

1 teaspoon Sweet Chilli Sauce (see page 38)
1 tablespoon rice vinegar
1 tablespoon lime juice
1 tablespoon olive oil
1 teaspoon fish sauce

Place a frying pan over medium heat. Brush the chicken with oil and season with Celtic salt and pepper. Place in the pan and cook until tender. Allow to cool then shred.

Place salad ingredients in a bowl and mix.

Fill a jar with a tight-fitting lid with the dressing ingredients and shake to combine. Pour over the salad and toss through. Serve in 2 bowls or place in 2 airtight containers to take to work for a midday meal.

NOTE: If you are in a hurry, you can use a ¼ of a cooked or barbecue chicken. Remove the skin and discard. Shred the chicken. This salad also makes a great filling for rice paper rolls.

Mid-afternoon snack

If you have eaten breakfast, fruit mid-morning and a midday meal, you may not need much fuel in the afternoon. Top up your digestive fire with a small protein snack. At this time of day, start reducing the carbohydrates you eat. This is only a snack so keep the quantities small. You could eat a handful of nuts, a hard-boiled egg, yoghurt, a healthy dip with vegetable sticks or a fruit smoothie.

- Mango smoothie
- Blueberry smoothie

Mango smoothie

Mangos are a super food providing vitamin A for healthy eyes and skin. They are rich in vitamin C and antioxidants and are also high in soluble fibre and lower cholesterol. When added to the yoghurt, this smoothie is full of enzymes that aid digestion and speed up the metabolism.

1 drink

½ cup natural yoghurt
1 teaspoon manuka honey
flesh of a small mango
¼ cup water
3 ice cubes

Place all ingredients in the jug of a blender and blend until smooth. Pour into a tall glass and enjoy.

Blueberry smoothie

Blueberries are a super food providing antioxidants and fiber for digestive health. They also lower blood sugar and cholesterol.

1 drink

½ cup natural yoghurt
1 teaspoon manuka honey
½ cup water
¾ cup frozen blueberries

Place all ingredients in the jug of a blender and blend until smooth. Pour into a tall glass and enjoy.

NOTE: You can also use a stick blender to make these smoothies.

Opposite page:
Blueberry smoothie, in front,
Mango smoothie, behind

Evening meals

Your metabolism naturally slows down at sunset so eat an early evening meal of protein and vegetables – the build-and-repair foods. Minimising your carbohydrates at this time will ensure that you do not store them as body fat while you sleep.

- Simple egg and salad dinner
- Spinach and ricotta pie with roasted beetroot (beet) salad
- Baked mushrooms with bean and pumpkin salad
- Roasted tofu and walnut salad
- Chickpea (garbanzo) and pumpkin curry with cucumber dip
- Bean and eggplant (aubergine) bake
- Vegetable stir-fry with almonds and quinoa
- Coq au vin with butter (lima) beans
- Corned beef with tomato relish and beans
- Slow-cooked lamb shanks with cannellini beans
- Yummy meatballs in homemade tomato sauce
- Thai fishcakes with Asian coleslaw
- Marinated chicken skewers with Japanese quinoa salad
- Lamb with fig and walnut salad
- Baked eggplants (aubergines) and fennel salad
- Lamb cutlets with grilled vegetable salad
- Poached salmon with sprouted salad
- Oven-baked salmon with Japanese salad
- Thai chicken balls with salad
- Thai squid with lemon and pea quinoa salad
- Beef and sweet potato casserole
- Ginger poached chicken with bean and pea salad
- Slow roasted beef with eggplant (aubergine) dip, roasted garlic and salad
- Baked capsicums (peppers) and salad
- Mexican chilli chicken
- Baked fish with avocado salsa
- Beef and greens with spiced pumpkin
- Chicken breast with quinoa tabouli and avocado
- Chicken and chickpea (garbanzo) stew

Simple egg and salad dinner

1 meal

This is a simple and quick meal for when you really don't have time to cook or if you arrive home very late of an evening.

> handful mixed salad leaves, washed and dried
> 4 cherry tomatoes, cut in half
> 4 slices Lebanese cucumber
> 1 tablespoon walnuts, chopped
> 1 sprig flat-leaf parsley, leaves only
> 1 tablespoon Mustard and Orange Salad Dressing
>   (see page 38)
> 2 free-range or organic eggs
> 1 tablespoon white vinegar
> Celtic sea salt
> cracked black pepper

Arrange salad ingredients in a bowl and toss with the dressing.

Break each egg into a cup to ensure the yolk is intact. Fill a deep-sided saucepan with at least 10 cm (4 in) of simmering water. Add the vinegar. Stir the water with a spoon, creating a small whirlpool. Drop each egg into the centre of the whirlpool and cook for 3 to 4 minutes. The water will settle and the eggs should form an oval. Remove the eggs with a slotted spoon, drain well and place on top of the salad. Season with Celtic salt and cracked black pepper and serve.

NOTE: Any of your favourite salad ingredients can be added. Walnuts are naturally high in melatonin and help you to relax into a good night's sleep.

Spinach and ricotta pie with roasted beetroot (beet) salad

6 meals

1 cup of rolled oats
¼ cup grated parmesan cheese
1 tablespoon spelt flour, white or wholemeal
pinch of Celtic sea salt, plus extra
50 g (1.75 oz) butter, melted
500 g (1.1 lb) fresh English spinach or baby spinach leaves
1 teaspoon olive oil
1 small leek (white part only), finely chopped
400 g (14 oz) fresh ricotta cheese
4 free-range or organic eggs, beaten lightly
2 tablespoons natural yoghurt
125 g (4.5 oz) feta cheese crumbled, (can also use goat's feta)
2 tablespoons grated parmesan cheese, extra
1 serve Roasted Beetroot (Beet) Salad per person (see page 47)

Preheat oven to 180°C (350°F). Grease and line a 20–22 cm (8–9 in) round spring-form tin.

Place rolled oats in a food processor and blend to breadcrumbs. Place in a small bowl with parmesan cheese, spelt flour, pinch of Celtic salt and melted butter. Mix well and press evenly over the base of a greased tin. Place the prepared tin in the refrigerator to chill for 10 minutes.

Steam spinach for 2 minutes. Drain and press out all the liquid from the spinach (this step is important). Chop roughly.

Heat the olive oil in a non-stick frying pan and sauté the leek for 2 minutes. Set aside to cool.

Mix ricotta, pinch of Celtic salt, eggs and yoghurt in a food processor or mixer and blend until smooth. Transfer to a large bowl and stir in crumbled feta, spinach and leek. Mix thoroughly and pour over crumb base. Sprinkle top with extra grated parmesan cheese.

Bake for 50 minutes with a piece of foil or baking paper over the pie to stop the top from burning. Remove foil or baking paper and bake uncovered for a further 10 minutes or until set.

Slice into six and serve with Roasted Beetroot (Beet) Salad.

NOTE: Can also be served cold the next day for tasty leftovers.

Baked mushrooms with bean and pumpkin salad

2 meals

1 teaspoon olive oil

1 small onion, finely chopped

2 garlic cloves, finely chopped

1 cup fresh breadcrumbs (preferably spelt)

50 g (1.75 oz) marinated goat's feta, crumbled (reserve oil)

8 walnut halves, finely chopped

1 teaspoon chopped flat-leaf parsley

2 pieces Preserved Lemon (see page 50), finely chopped or $\frac{1}{2}$ teaspoon finely grated lemon zest

pinch of Celtic sea salt and cracked black pepper

4 pieces Spiced Roasted Pumpkin (see page 42)

4 large mushrooms, stems removed

1 tablespoon grated parmesan cheese

1 quantity Bean and Pumpkin Salad

Preheat oven to 180°C (350°F).

Heat oil in a frying pan and cook the onion for 2 minutes, then add the garlic for 30 seconds. Transfer to a bowl and mix together with the breadcrumbs, goat's feta, walnuts, parsley, preserved lemon, Celtic salt and pepper.

Place the cooked pumpkin in another larger bowl and mash roughly with a fork. Add the other ingredients to the pumpkin and stir to mix.

Place the mushrooms cup side up on a tray lined with baking paper. Fill with the breadcrumb mixture and drizzle with a little oil from the marinated feta. Sprinkle with the parmesan cheese and bake for 15 to 20 minutes until the mushrooms soften and the breadcrumbs brown. Serve warm with the Bean and Pumpkin Salad.

Bean and pumpkin salad

16 green beans

8 sugar snap peas

6 pieces Spiced Roasted Pumpkin (see page 42)

$\frac{1}{2}$ cup tinned butter (lima) beans, rinsed

2 teaspoons marinated goat's feta, crumbled

1 teaspoon currants (optional)

1 teaspoon chopped flat-leaf parsley

olive oil, to drizzle

Celtic sea salt

cracked black pepper

Bring a small saucepan of water to the boil. Reduce to a simmer and cook the green beans for 1 minute, then add the sugar snap peas for a further 1 minute. Drain and run under cold water for 1 minute to halt the cooking.

Place in a medium-sized bowl. Add the pumpkin, butter (lima) beans, feta, currants and parsley and toss with a drizzle of olive oil. Season with Celtic salt and cracked black pepper.

Roasted tofu and walnut salad

1 meal

250 g (9 oz) firm tofu

1 tablespoon olive oil

4 tablespoons tamari

1 cup fresh orange juice

1 teaspoon Sweet Chilli Sauce (see page 38)

1 teaspoon grated ginger

1 tablespoon lemon juice

1 tablespoon mirin

½ red capsicum (pepper), cut into thin strips

½ small Lebanese cucumber, cut into thin strips

handful rocket (arugula) leaves or half a butter lettuce, washed and dried

handful bean sprouts

1 spring onion, thinly sliced

2 tablespoons walnuts, roughly chopped

4 Vietnamese mint leaves, thinly sliced

2 small mint leaves, thinly sliced

1 teaspoon sesame seeds

1 teaspoon sunflower seeds

Slice tofu into 8 square pieces and dry on paper towel.

Place a non-stick frying pan over high heat, add oil and tofu and fry until brown on all sides. Remove tofu and place in a small baking dish.

In a small bowl, combine tamari, orange juice, chilli sauce, ginger, lemon juice and mirin. Pour sauce over tofu. Cover and allow it to marinate in the refrigerator for 2 hours or ideally overnight.

Preheat oven to 180°C (350°F).

Bake tofu until the marinade reduces down to a sticky sauce. This will take approximately 40 minutes. Occasionally open the oven and spoon sauce over tofu while baking.

While the tofu is cooking, place a small, heavy pan over medium heat and lightly toast the sunflower and sesame seeds until they begin to brown. Remove from the heat and set aside.

In a serving bowl, gently mix together the capsicum (pepper), cucumber, salad leaves, bean sprouts, spring onion, walnuts, mint and roasted tofu. Pour the sticky sauce over the top of the salad and sprinkle with toasted seeds. Serve immediately.

Chickpea (garbanzo) and pumpkin curry with cucumber dip

3 meals

1 teaspoon olive oil

1 small brown onion, finely chopped

1 garlic clove, finely chopped

¼ cup dry white wine

1 heaped teaspoon grated ginger

1 teaspoon Favourite Spice Mix (see page 34)

1 teaspoon red curry paste

1 cup pumpkin, diced into 2 cm (¾ in) pieces

1 carrot, diced into 1 cm (½ in) pieces

1 small stick celery, diced into 1 cm (½ in)

1 x 400 g (14 oz) tin chickpeas (garbanzos), rinsed and drained

1 x 400 g (14 oz) tin diced tomatoes

2 cups vegetable stock

1 teaspoon tomato paste

3 handfuls baby spinach leaves, washed and dried

3 Spelt Chapatti (see page 40)

1 quantity Cucumber Dip

Heat olive oil in a pan over medium heat. Cook onion for 1 minute, then add garlic, white wine, ginger, spice mix, red curry paste, pumpkin, carrot, celery, chickpeas, tomatoes, vegetable stock and tomato paste. Cook on medium heat without a lid for 35 minutes or until the pumpkin and carrot are soft. Turn heat off and add spinach leaves. Stir through.

Place a non-stick frying pan over high heat and dry-fry the chapattis one at a time on both sides. To serve, spoon curry into bowls, top with cucumber dip and serve with 1 Spelt Chapatti per meal.

Cucumber dip

½ cup natural yoghurt

4 cm (1.5 in) length cucumber, grated

Combine ingredients in a small bowl.

Bean and eggplant (aubergine) bake

3 meals

1 large eggplant (aubergine), thinly sliced lengthwise (12 slices)

olive oil for brushing plus 1 tablespoon extra

$\frac{1}{2}$ leek (white part only), finely diced

1 garlic clove, finely chopped

1 stick celery, diced into 1 cm ($\frac{1}{2}$ in) pieces

1 small red capsicum (pepper), de-seeded and diced into 1 cm ($\frac{1}{2}$ in) pieces

1 x 400 g (14 oz) tin diced tomatoes or 1 $\frac{1}{2}$ cups Homemade Tomato Sauce (see page 53)

$\frac{1}{4}$ cup dry white wine

1 heaped teaspoon tomato paste

1 x 400 g (14 oz) tin cannellini beans, drained and rinsed

1 teaspoon Favourite Spice Mix (see page 34)

pinch of Celtic sea salt

Rosemary Flavour Bag (see page 34), optional

1 free-range or organic egg

$\frac{1}{4}$ cup natural yoghurt

1 tablespoon grated parmesan cheese

3 handfuls of mixed salad leaves, washed and dried

3 tablespoons Mustard and Orange Salad Dressing (see page 38)

Brush the eggplant (aubergine) slices with olive oil and grill. Drain on absorbent paper and set aside.

Preheat oven to 180°C (350°F).

Heat 1 tablespoon olive oil in a frying pan and add the leek, garlic, celery and capsicum (pepper) and cook for 3 minutes or until slightly softened. Add the tomatoes or Homemade Tomato Sauce, wine, tomato paste, cannellini beans, spice mix, Celtic salt and flavour bag. Bring to the boil and simmer for 10 minutes, stirring occasionally.

Remove flavour bag. Brush a deep ovenproof dish 22 x 13 cm (8.5 x 5 in) with olive oil. Layer four eggplant (aubergine) slices in the dish, overlapping them slightly.

Spoon half of the bean mixture on top. Repeat a second layer. Place four eggplant (aubergine) slices on top and gently press down to create a smooth surface.

In a separate, small bowl, whisk the egg and yoghurt together, then pour over the top. Sprinkle with the parmesan. Bake in oven for 30 minutes or until golden brown and bubbling. Toss the mixed salad leaves with the salad dressing and serve immediately with the bake.

NOTE: If you have time, use $\frac{1}{2}$ cup dried cannellini beans instead of canned beans. Soak in water overnight, drain, then simmer in fresh water until tender.

Vegetable stir-fry with almonds and quinoa

1 meal

1 tablespoon olive oil

½ small Spanish onion, thinly sliced

½ red capsicum (pepper) thinly sliced

125 g (4.5 oz) mixed vegetables, such as beans, broccolini (baby broccoli), bok choy, mushrooms or sugar snap peas

½ teaspoon of fresh ginger, finely shredded

½ red chilli, de-seeded and finely sliced or 1 teaspoon of Sweet Chilli Sauce (see page 38)

1 tablespoon of tamari

1 tablespoon lime juice

12 almonds

½ cup cooked quinoa (see page 56)

½ teaspoon finely grated lemon zest

1 tablespoon Mustard and Orange Salad Dressing (see page 38)

1 sprig fresh coriander (cilantro), leaves only

Heat the oil in a wok or heavy frying pan. Stir-fry the onion and capsicum (pepper) for 1 minute. Add the mixed vegetables, ginger, chilli, tamari, lime juice and almonds. Stir-fry for 2 minutes.

Place cooked quinoa in a small bowl and add the lemon zest and dressing. Stir to combine. Grease the inside of a small plastic cup and pack the quinoa into the cup, pressing down firmly. Place the cup upside down onto a plate and gently tap so that the quinoa forms a cup-like stack on the plate. Arrange the stir-fry next to the quinoa and top with fresh coriander (cilantro).

Coq au vin with butter (lima) beans

2 meals

300 g (10.5 oz) free-range or organic chicken thigh fillets,
   chopped into 2.5 cm (1 in) cubes
Celtic sea salt and cracked pepper
1 tablespoon olive oil
6 pickling onions, peeled and left whole
100 g (3.5 oz) button mushrooms
2 slices lean bacon, thinly sliced (optional)
4 garlic cloves, finely chopped
1 teaspoon tomato paste
1 cup dry red wine
1 cup chicken stock
2 bay leaves
2 sprigs of thyme
large handful of baby spinach leaves, washed and dried
½ x 400 g (14 oz) tin butter (lima) beans, rinsed and drained
1 teapoon chopped, flat-leaf parsley
1 bunch of broccolini (baby broccoli)
half an orange for squeezing

Preheat oven to 180°C (350°F).

Season chicken pieces with Celtic salt and pepper. Heat oil in a fry pan and add chicken pieces, browning on all sides. Remove chicken. Add onions, mushrooms, bacon and garlic to the pan and cook for 3 minutes. Add the tomato paste, wine and stock for another minute. Transfer to a casserole dish with a tight-fitting lid. Add the chicken, bay leaves and thyme. Put lid on casserole dish and bake in oven for 50 minutes.

Remove from oven. Take chicken pieces out and keep warm. Discard bay leaves and thyme. Place dish on high heat on stovetop and simmer uncovered for 3 minutes or until the juices reduce. If your casserole dish is not suitable to go on the stovetop, transfer the vegetables and juices to a pan and simmer for 3 minutes. Add the beans and spinach leaves and simmer for another 2 minutes.

Lightly steam the broccolini (baby broccoli) and squeeze the orange juice over top.

Place chicken onto 2 plates and top with the vegetable and bean sauce. Sprinkle with parsley and serve with steamed broccolini (baby broccoli).

NOTE: Use the left over butter (lima) beans in a salad for another meal.

Corned beef with tomato relish and beans

This recipe requires a slow cooker. When cooked, the corned beef can be sliced for another meal or used in wraps for lunches.

1 large onion, peeled and halved

2 bay leaves

2 cloves

½ teaspoon peppercorns

¼ cup dry white wine

1 tablespoon raw caster sugar

1 tablespoon white vinegar

1 carrot, sliced lengthways

1 kg (2.2 lbs) corned beef

green beans, 10 per person

Tomato Relish

In the dish of your slow cooker place the onion, bay leaves, cloves, peppercorns, wine, sugar, white vinegar and carrot.

Rinse the meat in cold water and place in the slow cooker. Cover with cold water and cook on slow heat for 2 hours. Take the lid off and turn the meat over. Replace the lid and cook for a further 2 hours.

Remove the meat, cover with foil and rest for 5 minutes. Discard the water and vegetables. Serve slices of the corned beef with streamed green beans and tomato relish.

Tomato relish

1 tablespoon olive oil

1 brown onion, finely chopped

1 garlic clove, finely chopped

500 g (1.1 lb) ripe tomatoes, finely chopped

1 long red chilli, finely chopped (de-seed for a milder relish)

1 tablespoon balsamic vinegar

1 tablespoon raw caster sugar

1 teaspoon currants

1 sprig thyme

pinch of Celtic sea salt and cracked black pepper

Heat oil in a medium saucepan and sauté the onions for 30 seconds then add the garlic and saute for another 30 seconds. Add remaining ingredients and bring to the boil. Reduce the heat and simmer for 25 minutes, stirring occasionally. Allow to cool.

Remove thyme sprig and transfer to a sterilised glass jar (see page 28 for instructions). Store in the refrigerator.

Slow-cooked lamb shanks with cannellini beans

2 meals

¼ cup dried cannellini beans, soaked overnight in cold water

2 lamb shanks

¼ cup white spelt flour

¼ teaspoon Celtic sea salt

1 teaspoon sweet paprika

1 tablespoon olive oil, plus extra 1 tablespoon

1 small brown onion, finely chopped

4 garlic cloves, finely chopped

1 celery stalk, finely chopped

1 small carrot, roughly chopped into 2 cm (¾ in) pieces

1 small sweet potato roughly chopped, into 2 cm (¾ in) pieces

1 cup dry red wine

1 Rosemary Flavour Bag (see page 34)

2 sprigs of thyme

2 bay leaves

½ x 400 g (14 oz) tin diced tomatoes

1 teaspoon tomato paste

2 cups beef stock

pinch of cracked black pepper

1 teaspoon chopped, flat-leaf parsley

2 serves Green Vegetable Medley (see page 52)

olive oil, to drizzle

half an orange or lemon

Be sure to soak the cannellini beans overnight in cold water before starting this recipe.

Preheat oven to 180°C (350°F).

Mix the flour, Celtic salt and paprika in a plastic bag. Add the lamb shanks and shake to coat with the flour mixture.

Heat 1 tablespoon olive oil in a large pan and cook the shanks until browned on all sides. Transfer to a large casserole dish. Add remaining 1 tablespoon oil to the large pan and cook the onion, garlic, celery, carrot and sweet potato for 3 minutes. Add the wine and simmer for 2 minutes, then add flavour bag, thyme, bay leaves, tomatoes, tomato paste, stock and pepper and turn off heat.

Drain the cannellini beans and add uncooked to the pan, mixing all ingredients together. Transfer this mixture to the casserole dish with the lamb shanks. Cover with a lid or foil and transfer to the oven. Braise for 3 hours. Discard the flavour bag, bay leaves and thyme.

When cooking time is nearly complete, lightly steam the Green Vegetable Medley. Drizzle with olive oil and squeeze over the orange or lemon juice. Place shanks onto serving plates and ladle the sauce on top. Sprinkle with the chopped parsley and serve with the Green Vegetable Medley.

NOTE: Freeze the other half of the tinned tomatoes.

Yummy meatballs with homemade tomato sauce

2 meals

250 g (9 oz) lean beef mince
½ onion, finely chopped
1 garlic clove, finely chopped
½ teaspoon Favourite Spice Mix (see page 34)
1 free-range or organic egg, lightly beaten
½ cup fresh ricotta cheese
¼ cup fresh breadcrumbs (preferably spelt)
1 tablespoon chopped flat-leaf parsley
pinch of Celtic sea salt
cracked black pepper
1 teaspoon olive oil
1 cup Homemade Tomato Sauce (see page 53)
½ butter lettuce, leaves washed and dried
6 cherry tomatoes cut in half
8 slices cucumber
2 tablespoons Mustard and Orange Salad Dressing (see page 38)
1 teaspoon chopped, flat-leaf parsley, extra

In a medium bowl mix the beef mince, onion, garlic, spice mix, egg, ricotta cheese, breadcrumbs, 1 tablespoon parsley, Celtic salt and cracked black pepper. It is easier to use your hands. Take tablespoons of the mixture and roll into meatballs. Chill them in the refrigerator for 15 minutes.

Heat olive oil in a pan and cook the meatballs for 10 minutes, browning on all sides. Add the tomato sauce and cook gently for another 5 minutes.

Arrange the lettuce, cherry tomatoes and cucumber slices in a small bowl. Drizzle dressing over the salad and set aside.

Divide the meatballs between 2 bowls and spoon the tomato sauce over the top. Sprinkle with the extra parsley and serve with the salad.

Thai fishcakes with Asian coleslaw

1 meal + extra Asian coleslaw for another meal

180 g (6.5 oz) salmon steak with skin and bones removed, roughly chopped

1 small free-range or organic egg, lightly beaten (only use half)

1 teaspoon Thai red curry paste

½ teaspoon Sweet Chilli Sauce (see page 38)

1 teaspoon fish sauce

1 tablespoon chopped fresh coriander (cilantro)

½ cup fresh breadcrumbs, preferably spelt

2 teaspoons spelt flour, for shaping patties

1–2 tablespoons olive oil

1 cup Asian Coleslaw

¼ cup Lemon Mayonnaise (see page 38)

Place the salmon, egg, curry paste, chilli sauce, fish sauce and coriander (cilantro) in a food processor and pulse for a few seconds. Do not over mix. Stir through the breadcrumbs. Place in refrigerator to chill for 15 minutes.

Flour your hands and shape the mixture into three fish cakes. Cover and chill for 20 minutes to firm up.

Heat the oil in a fry pan over high heat and cook the fishcakes for 3 minutes on each side until golden. Serve with Asian Coleslaw and Lemon Mayonnaise.

NOTE: The fishcakes can be made up the night before and left in the refrigerator until required.

Asian coleslaw

½ cup red cabbage, finely shredded

½ cup Chinese cabbage, finely shredded

1 small carrot, cut into matchsticks

1 spring onion, thinly sliced

5 Vietnamese mint leaves, torn

¼ cup coriander (cilantro) leaves

¼ cup chopped walnuts

4 sugar snap peas, thinly sliced

2 tablespoons Mustard and Orange Salad Dressing (see page 38)

In a large serving bowl, combine all the coleslaw ingredients and toss the dressing through. Cover and set aside in a cool place.

NOTE: Enjoy the left over Asian Coleslaw as a midday meal with a small can of tuna or salmon.

Marinated chicken skewers with Japanese quinoa salad

2 meals

6 tablespoons tamari

2 tablespoons mirin

½ cup freshly squeezed orange juice

1 teaspoon freshly grated ginger

1 tablespoon Sweet Chilli Sauce (see page 38)

1 tablespoon manuka honey

400 g (14 oz) free-range or organic chicken breast, cut into 2 cm (¾ in) pieces

4 bamboo skewers

1 quantity Japanese Quinoa Salad (see page 126)

Put the tamari, mirin, orange juice, ginger, chilli sauce and honey into a small saucepan and bring to the boil. Reduce to a simmer and cook for 8 minutes, stirring occasionally until the mixture becomes syrupy. Set aside to cool.

Thread 5 to 6 pieces of chicken onto each skewer and place in a shallow casserole dish lined with baking paper. When cool, pour the sticky marinade over the chicken skewers and turn to coat the chicken. Cover and chill for a couple of hours or ideally overnight.

Preheat oven to 180°C (350°F).

Bake the chicken skewers in the shallow casserole dish for 10 minutes. Turn the chicken skewers over and spoon over the sauce. Bake for another 5 minutes and serve with the Japanese Quinoa Salad.

NOTE: I find it convenient to marinate the chicken on shopping day and either use the next day or freeze. The chicken skewers can be baked or cooked on a barbeque. If using a barbecue, soak bamboo skewers in water for 30 minutes before threading on the chicken. This prevents the bamboo from burning with the heat of the barbecue.

Japanese quinoa salad

½ cup cooked quinoa (see page 56)

2 sheets nori, torn into bite size pieces

1 spring onion, thinly sliced

8 cm (3 in) piece cucumber, cut into small cubes

½ red capsicum (pepper), finely chopped

2 tablespoons cooked green peas

¼ cup chopped flat-leaf parsley

1 tablespoon Sweet Chilli Sauce (see page 38)

1 tablespoon rice vinegar

2 tablespoons lime juice

2 tablespoons olive oil

1 teaspoon sesame seeds

In a medium-sized bowl, add quinoa, nori, spring onion, cucumber, red capsicum (pepper), peas and parsley. In a glass jar with a tight-fitting lid mix together chilli sauce, rice vinegar, lime juice, olive oil and sesame seeds. Pour over the quinoa salad and toss to mix.

Lamb with fig and walnut salad

1 meal

1 x 150–200 g (5.5–7oz) lamb backstrap or lamb steak

olive oil for brushing

Celtic sea salt and cracked black pepper

1 large fresh fig

¼ bunch watercress or rocket (arugula) leaves, washed and dried

6 walnuts, roughly chopped

50 g (1.75 oz) marinated goat's feta, crumbled (reserve oil)

Brush the lamb with the olive oil and season with the Celtic salt and pepper. Heat a grill pan and cook the lamb on all sides until browned and cooked to your taste. Set aside to rest.

To make the salad, tear up the fig and add to a bowl with the watercress or rocket leaves, walnuts and marinated goat's feta. Drizzle with the reserved oil and toss to mix. Pile salad onto a plate. Slice the lamb into 3 or 4 pieces and arrange on the salad.

Opposite page:
Lamb with fig and
walnut salad

Baked eggplants (aubergines) and fennel salad

4 meals

2 eggplants (aubergines), cut in half length ways
olive oil, for cooking
Celtic sea salt and cracked pepper
1 small onion, finely chopped
2 garlic cloves, finely chopped
250 g (9 oz) lean beef mince
¼ cup white wine, optional
½ cup Homemade Tomato Sauce (see page 53)
Rosemary Flavour Bag (see page 34)
1 teaspoon chopped flat-leaf parsley
1 free-range or organic egg, beaten
½ cup Greek yoghurt
2 tablespoons grated parmesan cheese
4 serves Fennel Salad (see page 129)

Using a sharp knife, cut a crisscross pattern into the white flesh of the eggplant (aubergine). Remove the flesh with a spoon leaving 1 cm around edges to form a shell. Heat 1 tablespoon olive oil in a medium-sized frying pan and add the eggplant (aubergine) flesh. Cook for 8 minutes or until tender and golden. Season with Celtic salt and pepper and set aside.

Return the pan to the heat, add 1 teaspoon olive oil and cook onion for 2 minutes, then add the garlic and cook for 1 minute stirring continually. Add the beef mince and cook until browned. Add the wine, tomato sauce, flavour bag and cook for 20 minutes with the lid on. Stir occasionally. Remove from the heat and discard the flavour bag. Add the parsley and cooked eggplant (aubergine).

Preheat oven to 180°C (350°F). Line a baking tray with baking paper.

Heat a large pan with 1 tablespoon of olive oil and grill the eggplants (aubergines) on each side to brown the surface. Then place on baking tray, cut side up and fill with meat mixture.

In a small bowl, gently mix the beaten egg into the yoghurt. Spoon over the top of the filled eggplants (aubergines) and top with grated parmesan cheese. Bake for 30 minutes, or until the eggplants (aubergines) are tender and golden. Serve with Fennel Salad.

NOTE: You can use ½ cup of pureed tomatoes if you do not have Homemade Tomato Sauce.

Fennel salad

1 serve

½ butter lettuce, washed and dried
¼ fennel bulb, thinly sliced
1 small orange
4 mint leaves, thinly sliced
¼ cup baby olives
olive oil, to drizzle
Celtic sea salt and cracked black
    pepper

Arrange the lettuce leaves in a bowl with the fennel slices.

Using a sharp knife, peel the orange and remove the white pith. Cut the orange into thin segments and add to the salad with the mint leaves and olives. Toss together with a drizzle of olive oil and season with Celtic salt and cracked black pepper.

Lamb cutlets with grilled vegetable salad

Serves 2

6 lamb cutlets
olive oil, for brushing
1 teaspoon Favourite Spice Mix
    (see page 34)
1 medium green zucchini (courgette)
2 oriental eggplants (aubergines)
1 red capsicum (pepper)
½ Spanish onion
handful of rocket (arugula) leaves,
    washed and dried
1 sprig flat-leaf parsley, leaves only

Brush the lamb cutlets with olive oil and rub with the spice mix. Set aside to marinate.

Slice zucchini and eggplants (aubergines) lengthways into thin slices. Cut capsicum (pepper)into quarters and discard the seeds and membranes. Cut onion into 4 wedges.

Heat a grill pan or a large frying pan. Brush the vegetables with olive oil and cook in batches until tender and browned. Drain on paper towels.

Heat a heavy frying pan and cook the lamb cutlets for 2 minutes each side. Remove and set aside to rest.

Combine all vegetables and rocket (arugula) leaves in a large bowl with parsley. To serve, pile the roasted vegetables in a high stack onto plates and top with the lamb cutlets.

Poached salmon with sprouted salad

1 meal

150–180 g (5.5–6.5 oz) salmon steak, bones removed
½ teaspoon miso paste
1 cup hot water
2 teaspoons sunflower seeds
1 teaspoon sesame seeds
4 sugar snap peas, cut into matchsticks
½ red capsicum (pepper), white pith removed and cut
    into matchsticks
1 spring onion, thinly sliced on the diagonal
4 slices cucumber
25 g (1 oz) marinated goat's feta, crumbled
handful of rocket (arugula) leaves, washed and dried
handful mixed sprouts (alfalfa, radish, red clover,
    chickpea (garbanzo)

For the dressing

1 tablespoon lime juice
1 teaspoon Sweet Chilli Sauce (see page 38)
1 tablespoon olive oil
pinch of Celtic sea salt

Place a small pan with a fitted lid over medium heat. Dissolve the miso in the hot water and place in the pan. Bring to a simmer and gently lower the salmon into the pan. Put the lid on and poach the salmon for 5 minutes or until cooked.

While the salmon is cooking, place a small, heavy pan over medium heat and lightly toast the sunflower and sesame seeds until they begin to brown. Remove from the heat and set aside.

Place snow peas, capsicum (pepper), spring onion, cucumber, feta, rocket (arugula) and mixed sprouts in a medium-sized bowl. Add the seeds and mix through.

Place dressing ingredients in a jar with a tight-fitting lid. Shake to combine and toss through salad.

Use an egg slice to gently remove the salmon from the pan. Break the salmon into chunks and discard the skin. Add to the salad and gently mix through. Pile onto a plate and serve immediately.

Oven-baked salmon with Japanese salad

1 meal

½ butter lettuce, leaves washed and dried

handful of watercress leaves, washed and dried

4 cherry tomatoes, halved

150–180 g (5.5–6.5 oz) salmon fillet, bones removed

Celtic sea salt and cracked pepper

4 sugar snap peas

6 whole pea pods

1 Yoghurt Cheese Ball (see page 44) or 25 g (1 oz)
     marinated goat's feta

For the dressing

½ teaspoon tamari

1 teaspoon miso paste dissolved in 1 tablespoon hot water

2 tablespoons mirin

1 tablespoon lime juice

1 teaspoon manuka honey

Preheat oven to 180°C (350°F).

Arrange lettuce, watercress and tomatoes in a shallow bowl.

Place the salmon on a baking tray lined with baking paper. Season
with Celtic salt and pepper. Bake for 6 to 8 minutes depending on
how pink you like your salmon.

Steam or blanch the sugar snap peas and whole pea pods for two
minutes. Add to the salad. (You can either pod the peas or eat
them whole.)

Break the salmon into chunks and discard the skin. Add the salmon
to the salad and gently mix through. Pile onto a plate.

Place the dressing ingredients in a small jar with a tight-fitting lid.
Shake to mix and drizzle over salad. Top with Yoghurt Cheese Ball
or feta. Serve immediately.

Thai chicken balls with salad

2 meals

1 x 200 g (7 oz) free-range or organic chicken breast, roughly chopped

½ cup fresh breadcrumbs

1 teaspoon fish sauce

1 spring onion, finely sliced

2 tablespoons chopped coriander (cilantro)

1 teaspoon grated ginger

1 free-range or organic egg, beaten

1 teaspoon chopped red chilli or Sweet Chilli Sauce (see page 38)

pinch of Celtic sea salt

pinch of cracked pepper

1 tablespoon olive oil, for frying

For the dressing

1 teaspoon Sweet Chilli Sauce (see page 38)

1 tablespoon rice vinegar

1 tablespoon lime juice

1 tablespoon olive oil

1 teaspoon fish sauce

For the salad

Handful bean sprouts

1 spring onion, finely sliced on the diagonal

½ cup Chinese cabbage, finely shredded

6 Vietnamese mint leaves, torn

½ small Lebanese cucumber, cut into matchsticks

¼ cup Asian basil leaves, torn

½ red capsicum (pepper), thinly sliced

Place the chicken breast in a food processor and mince. Transfer to a bowl and add the rest of the meatball ingredients except for the oil for frying. Mix together using your hands and roll into walnut-sized balls. Place on a tray and chill in the refrigerator for 15 minutes.

Heat the olive oil in a fry pan and cook the meatballs for 10 to 12 minutes or until browned and cooked. Set aside.

Place the dressing ingredients in a jar with a tight-fitting lid and shake to combine. To make the salad, toss together all ingredients with the dressing. Pile salad into 2 bowls and top with cooked Thai Chicken Balls. Serve immediately.

Thai squid with lemon, pea and quinoa salad

2 meals

4 squid hoods, approximately 400 g (14 oz)
olive oil, for brushing
½ small red chilli, finely diced
Celtic sea salt and cracked black pepper
handful coriander (cilantro) leaves
handful rocket (arugula) leaves
1 mango, peeled and sliced
lime wedges to serve

For the dressing
1 teaspoon Sweet Chilli Sauce (see page 38)
1 tablespoon lime juice
1 tablespoon olive oil
1 teaspoon fish sauce

Wash the squid hoods under cold running water. Pat dry with paper towels. Cut one side of each hood and lay flat. Lightly score the inside surface with a sharp knife, creating a criss-cross pattern, making sure you don't cut all the way through. Then slice the prepared squid into 5 cm (2 in) pieces and brush with olive oil. Season with red chilli, Celtic salt and pepper. Set aside to marinate for 15 minutes.

Arrange rocket (arugula), coriander and mango on two plates. Place dressing ingredients in a small jar with a tight-fitting lid and shake to combine. Make the Lemon, Pea and Quinoa Salad.

Heat a large grill pan. Cook squid in batches, scored side down first until cooked, about 4 minutes. Drain on paper towels. Place cooked squid on mango salad and drizzle over the dressing. Serve immediately with lime wedges and Lemon and Pea Quinoa Salad.

Place dressing ingredients in a small jar with a tight-fitting lid and shake to combine.

Lemon, pea and quinoa salad

1 cup cooked quinoa (see page 56)
2 pieces Preserved Lemon, diced (see page 50) or ½ teaspoon finely grated lemon zest
½ cup cooked peas
1 spring onion including green stem, finely chopped
1 tablespoon chopped mint leaves
2 Vietnamese mint leaves, finely chopped
1 tablespoon chopped, flat-leaf parsley
olive oil, to drizzle
juice of 1 lime
pinch of Celtic sea salt and cracked black pepper

Place all ingredients in a small bowl and stir to combine.

Beef and sweet potato casserole

I find osso bucco to be the most flavoursome meat for stews – the bones add depth of flavour. Do eat the marrow from the cooked bone because it is full of iron.

2–3 meals

½ cup cannellini beans, soaked overnight in cold water
1 teaspoon olive oil
500 g (1.1 lb) osso bucco steak, cut into large cubes
2 garlic cloves, finely chopped
½ cup dry red wine
1 sprig thyme
2 bay leaves
1 teaspoon Favourite Spice Mix (see page 34)
1 teaspoon tomato paste
½ x 400 g (14 oz) tin diced tomatoes
1½ cups beef stock
10 cm (4 in) piece sweet potato, cut into 4 large chunks
1 carrot, cut into 4 large chunks
10 small pickling onions, peeled and left whole
20 green beans
1 teaspoon chopped, flat-leaf parsley

Preheat the oven to 180°C (350°F).

Heat the olive oil in a large heavy pan and brown the meat on all sides. Add the garlic and cook for a minute. Pour the wine into the pan and simmer for 2 minutes.

Transfer to a casserole dish and add thyme, bay leaves, spice mix, tomato paste, diced tomatoes, beef stock, sweet potato and carrot. Drain the cannellini beans and add uncooked to the casserole. Give it a stir and put the lid on or cover with foil and bake in oven for 2 hours.

Add the onions at this stage, cover and cook for another 1 hour. Adding the onions after 2 hours allows them to hold their shape.

Just before serving, lightly steam the green beans. Remove the bay leaves and thyme and serve in bowls with the green beans. Sprinkle parsley on top.

NOTE: Freeze the other half of the tinned tomatoes.

Ginger poached chicken with bean and pea salad

2 meals

2 x 200 g (7 oz) free-range or organic chicken breasts

2 cups cold water

¼ cup dry white wine

1 large slice ginger

100 g (3.5 oz) fresh peas, podded

200 g (7 oz) broad (fava) beans podded

8 mint leaves, torn

8 cherry tomatoes, cut into quarters

½ teaspoon finely grated lemon zest

juice ½ lemon

4 Yoghurt Cheese Balls (see page 44) or 4 tablespoons marinated goat's feta, broken into pieces (reserve oil)

cracked black pepper and Celtic sea salt

6 baby cos (romaine) lettuce leaves, washed and dried

Place chicken breasts, water, wine and ginger in a small saucepan and heat up until the water is boiling. Take the pan off the heat and cover with a tight-fitting lid. The chicken continues to cook as the water cools down. After 10 minutes, test the chicken to see if it is cooked. If the chicken breasts are large, they may need another 5 minutes in the water with the lid on.

While the chicken is poaching, make the bean and pea salad. Bring a small saucepan of water to a simmer. Cook the broad (fava) beans in the water for 2 to 3 minutes and remove with a slotted spoon. Rinse in cold water to halt the cooking. Peel the skins and set aside. Cook the peas for 1 to 2 minutes. Drain and rinse in cold water.

In a bowl, combine the peas, broad (fava) beans, mint leaves, cherry tomatoes, lemon zest and juice, Yoghurt Cheese Balls or goat's feta, oil from cheese and Celtic salt and pepper. Spoon mixture into the cos (romaine) lettuce leaves and divide between 2 plates. Slice the chicken into thin strips and pile on the 2 plates.

Slow roasted beef with eggplant (aubergine) dip, roasted garlic and salad

This recipe requires a slow cooker. The slow cooking guarantees succulent meat.

- 1 large brown onion with skin on, halved
- 2 bay leaves
- ¼ cup dry white wine
- 1 sprig rosemary
- 1 carrot, sliced
- 1 teaspoon whole peppercorns
- 1 cup beef stock
- 1 kg (2.2 lb) beef
- handful of mixed salad leaves, washed and dried
- 2 tablespoons Mustard and Orange Salad Dressing (see page 38)
- 1 quantity of Eggplant (Aubergine) Dip
- 2 Roasted Garlic Bulbs, (see page 38)

In the dish of your slow cooker place the onion, bay leaves, wine, rosemary, carrot, peppercorns and beef stock. Place the meat on top. Cover with the lid and cook on low for 2 hours. Take the lid off and turn the meat over. Replace the lid and cook for a further 2 hours. Remove the meat, cover with foil and rest for 5 minutes.

Toss the salad leaves with the Mustard and Orange Salad Dressing. Serve slices of the beef with Eggplant (Aubergine) Dip, Roasted Garlic and salad.

NOTE: The leftover beef can be sliced and used in wraps for lunches or cold meat and salad dinners.

Eggplant (aubergine) dip

- 1 large eggplant (aubergine)
- 1 small garlic clove, crushed
- juice of ½ lemon
- 1 tablespoon tahini
- ¼ teaspoon ground cumin
- pinch of Celtic sea salt
- 2 tablespoons natural yoghurt

Preheat oven to 180°C.

Prick the eggplant (aubergine) with a skewer and place on a tray in the oven. The eggplant (aubergine) is cooked when it is soft to the touch. Remove from the oven, place in a bowl and cover with plastic. Set aside to cool.

Halve the eggplant (aubergine) and scoop out the flesh. Place in a food processor with garlic, lemon juice, tahini, cumin and Celtic salt and blend until smooth. Taste and add more Celtic salt or lemon juice according to your taste. Then gently stir through yoghurt with a spoon.

NOTE: You can use a Roasted Garlic clove instead of raw garlic for a richer flavour.

Baked capsicums (peppers) and salad

4 meals

1 teaspoon olive oil
1 small brown onion, finely diced
1 garlic clove, finely chopped
250 g (9 oz) lean beef mince
¼ cup dry white wine
1 teaspoon tomato paste
¾ cup Homemade Tomato Sauce (see page 53) or ½ x tin diced
   tomatoes
1 cup beef stock
1 teaspoon Favourite Spice Mix (see page 34)
½ x 400 g (14 oz) tin red kidney beans, rinsed and drained
2 large red capsicums (peppers), halved and de-seeded
¼ cup grated parmesan cheese
4 serves of Fresh and Crisp Salad (see page 47)

Heat the oil in a deep-sided pan and sauté the onions and garlic
for 1 minute. Add the beef mince and cook until browned. Add the
wine, tomato paste, tomato sauce or tomatoes, beef stock and
spice mix. Stir to mix and simmer for about 15 to 20 minutes,
stirring occasionally. Add kidney beans and stir through. Let the
mix cool slightly.

Preheat oven to 180°C (350°F). Line a baking tray with baking paper.

Spoon mixture into capsicum (pepper) halves and pack tightly.
Sprinkle the top with parmesan cheese and place on an oven tray.
Bake for 35 to 40 minutes or until capsicums (peppers) are tender.
Serve with Fresh and Crisp Salad.

NOTE: Freeze the other half of the tinned tomatoes. You can use any
bolognaise sauce for this recipe and add half a can of rinsed and
drained kidney beans. You may cook spaghetti bolognaise for the
family and the baked capsicums (peppers) are a no-carb meal for
you. Any leftovers can be reheated for a midday meal the next day.

Mexican chilli chicken

2–3 meals

1 tablespoon olive oil

400 g (14 oz) free-range or organic chicken thigh fillets, cut into 2 cm (¾ in) chunks

1 small onion, finely chopped

1 red capsicum (pepper), chopped into 1 cm (½ inch) dice

2 garlic cloves, finely chopped

½ teaspoon chilli powder

1 teaspoon Sweet Chilli Sauce (see page 38)

½ teaspoon sweet paprika

½ teaspoon ground cumin

1 x 400 g (14 oz) tin chopped tomatoes or 1½ cups Homemade Tomato Sauce (see page 53)

1 cup chicken stock

1 teaspoon tomato paste

1 x 400 g (14 oz) tin red kidney beans, rinsed and drained

1 Chapatti per meal (see page 39)

1 sprig flat-leaf parsley, leaves only

Heat the olive in a large pan and cook the chicken pieces until browned. Remove from the pan and set aside.

Add the onion and capsicum (pepper) to the pan and cook for 2 minutes. Add the garlic and stir with a wooden spoon for 1 minute. Add the chilli powder, chilli sauce, paprika, cumin, tomatoes or tomato sauce, chicken stock, tomato paste and cooked chicken and bring to a simmer. Cook for 20 minutes uncovered then add the kidney beans. Simmer for another 5 minutes.

Place a non-stick frying pan over high heat and dry-fry each chapatti on both sides.

To serve, spoon Chilli Chicken into bowls, top with parsley and serve with 1 Spelt Chapatti per meal.

Baked fish with avocado salsa

2 meals

1 whole snapper, approximately 500 g (1.1 lb)
1 tablespoon olive oil, for brushing
2 pieces Preserved Lemon (see page 50)
2 thyme sprigs
Celtic sea salt and cracked black pepper
half a lemon, for squeezing
handful of rocket (arugula) leaves, washed and dried
lemon wedges, to serve

For the avocado salsa

1 ripe avocado, diced
50 g (1.75 oz) marinated goat's feta, crumbled
1 small Lebanese cucumber, finely chopped
½ spring onion, finely sliced
1 sprig coriander (cilantro), leaves only
2 cm (¾ in) length lemongrass white part only, finely sliced
1 teaspoon Sweet Chilli Sauce (see page 38)
½ teaspoon fish sauce
1 teaspoon lime juice
1 teaspoon lemon juice
1 tablespoon olive oil

Preheat oven to 180°C (350°F).

Using a sharp knife, put 2 slashes in the skin of the fish on the top side. Brush the fish on both sides with olive oil. Place in a baking dish lined with baking paper.

In the cavity of the fish, place 2 pieces of preserved lemon and 2 thyme sprigs. Season the fish with Celtic salt and pepper. Squeeze lemon juice over fish. Bake for 15 to 20 minutes. It is cooked when the flesh in the slashes turns white or flakes when touched with a fork.

To make the salsa, place the avocado, goat's feta, cucumber, spring onion and coriander (cilantro) in a small bowl.

In a small jar with a tight-fitting lid, place lemongrass, chilli sauce, fish sauce, lime juice, lemon juice and olive oil and mix well. Pour over the salad and gently mix, being careful not to mash the avocado.

When fish is cooked, serve immediately with rocket (arugula) leaves, lemon wedges and avocado salsa.

Beef and greens with spiced pumpkin

1 meal

½ cup dry red wine

1 garlic clove, finely chopped

150–200 g (5.5–7 oz) of lean meat (eye fillet, porterhouse or rump)

3 pieces Spiced Pumpkin (see page 42)

Celtic salt and cracked black pepper

olive oil for brushing

3 pieces of broccolini (baby broccoli)

6 green beans

6 long slices of zucchini (courgette)

3 kale leaves (Tuscan cabbage)

1 Yoghurt Cheese Ball (see page 44) or 1 tablespoon marinated goat's feta

Combine the wine and chopped garlic and use to marinate the meat for 3 hours or preferably overnight.

Preheat oven to 180°C (350°F) and reheat or cook the pumpkin.

Remove the steaks from the marinade and dry with paper towels. Discard the marinade. Brush the steaks with olive oil and season with Celtic salt and cracked black pepper. Heat a grill pan over high heat for 5 minutes then cook the steaks for 4 to 5 minutes on each side. Remove from the pan and let rest for 4 to 5 minutes.

Lightly steam the green vegetables and drain. Arrange on serving plate. Place Yoghurt Cheese Ball or goat's feta on top and drizzle with a little of the oil. Thinly slice the meat and place on serving plates with the pumpkin and green vegetables.

Chicken breast with quinoa tabouli and avocado

1 meal + extra tabouli for another meal

200 g (7 oz) free-range or organic chicken breast
olive oil, for brushing
Celtic salt and cracked pepper
½ avocado, sliced thinly
¾ cup Quinoa Tabouli
1 iceberg lettuce leaf

Heat a non-stick frying pan or grill plate.

Brush the chicken breast on both sides with the olive oil and season with Celtic salt and cracked black pepper. Place in pan. When cooked, slice into 3 or 4 pieces and serve with the avocado slices and ¾ cup of quinoa tabouli placed in the iceberg lettuce leaf.

Quinoa tabouli

½ cup cooked quinoa (see page 56)
½ cup chopped flat-leaf parsley
1 tablespoon chopped mint
2 spring onions chopped finely, including the green tops
1 large tomato, de-seeded and diced
1 small garlic clove, finely chopped
1 tablespoon currants (optional)
juice of 1 lemon
1 piece Preserved Lemon (see page 50), finely chopped or
    ½ teaspoon finely grated lemon zest
¼ teaspoon cumin
2 tablespoons olive oil
Celtic sea salt and cracked pepper

Toss all ingredients in a bowl and mix well.

Chicken and chickpea (garbanzo) stew

2 meals

1 tablespoon olive oil

4 chicken drumsticks, approximately 600 g (21 oz), skin removed

1 red onion, thinly sliced

1 red capsicum (pepper), thinly sliced

2 garlic cloves, finely chopped

½ cup Homemade Tomato Sauce (see page 53) or ½ cup diced, tinned tomatoes

½ cup dry white wine

1 cup chicken stock

1 teaspoon Favourite Spice Mix (see page 34)

2 strips orange zest

2 sprigs fresh thyme

½ x 400 g (14 oz) tin chickpeas (garbanzos), rinsed and drained

20 baby olives

pinch of Celtic sea salt and cracked black pepper

1 teaspoon chopped flat-leaf parsley

2 serves of Fresh and Crisp Salad (see page 47)

Preheat oven to 180°C (350°F).

Heat the olive oil in a large frying pan and brown the chicken on both sides. Transfer chicken to a casserole dish.

Add the onions and capsicum (pepper) to the pan and cook for 2 minutes. Add the garlic and cook for another 1 minute. Remove from the pan using a slotted spoon and place in the casserole dish.

Add the tomato sauce or diced tomatoes, wine, chicken stock, spice mix, orange zest, thyme, chickpeas (garbanzos) and olives to the casserole. Give it a little stir and season with Celtic salt and pepper. Put lid on casserole or cover with foil and bake for 50 minutes.

When cooked, divide chicken between 2 bowls and ladle vegetables over the top. Sprinkle with the chopped parsley. Serve with Fresh and Crisp Salad.

NOTE: You may have enough sauce left over to have as a light meal with ¼ cup cooked quinoa the next day.

Treats

There are many reasons why sugar is of no benefit to your health but for many people, giving up sugar altogether is unrealistic and can lead to bingeing.

A more balanced approach is to be more discerning about your choice of treats. The following recipes include ingredients that offer nourishment. A small amount of these treats will satisfy because protein is included in the ingredients. Sharing an occasional treat with friends can then be a delight rather than a guilt-ridden choice.

If a recipe is too sweet for you, simply reduce the amount of sugar.

• Amaretti cookies
• Amaretti crumble
• Poached pears with amaretti crumble and ricotta crème
• Vanilla yoghurt with passionfruit and amaretti crumble
• Chocolate berry tart with ricotta crème
• Almond and blueberry muffins
• Ricotta chocolate mousse cake
• Date and almond flan
• Cherry cheesecakes
• Fruit and nut fudge
• Raisin cookies

Amaretti cookies

Makes 15

2 free-range or organic eggs, whites only
½ teaspoon vanilla essence
175 g (6 oz) almond meal
125 g (4.5 oz) raw caster sugar

Preheat oven to 180°C (350°F). Line an oven tray with baking paper.

In a medium-sized bowl, beat the egg whites until soft peaks form. Add vanilla and mix through.

In a separate bowl, mix together the almond meal and sugar. With a rubber spatula, gently fold the egg whites into the almond meal and sugar. The mixture will be very sticky.

Using your hands, roll the mixture into walnut-sized balls and place on the prepared oven tray. Depending on how sticky your mixture is, you may need to slightly flour your hands, or you can simply drop teaspoons of the mixture onto the baking tray. Bake for 20 to 25 minutes or until golden. Cool on a cake rack.

NOTE: Egg yolks can be used to make mayonnaise. (see page 38)

Amaretti crumble

4 Amaretti Cookies, broken into pieces
½ teaspoon allspice
25 g (1 oz) butter

Preheat oven to 180°C (350°F). Line a baking tray with baking paper.

Place all ingredients in a food processor and pulse into large crumbs. Tip onto prepared oven tray and spread out evenly using your fingers. Bake for 8 to 10 minutes until golden brown and remove from the oven. Set aside to cool and then break the biscuit mixture into crumbs with your hands.

NOTE: Amaretti crumble can be stored in an airtight container for 2 weeks. It is delicious with any poached fruit. Try poaching apricots, peaches or nectarines.

Opposite page:
Amaretti cookies

Poached pears with amaretti crumble and ricotta crème

2 treats

½ cup dry marsala or sweet dessert wine

1 cup organic apple juice

1 vanilla bean, split

1 cinnamon stick

2 small pears

2 tablespoons Amaretti Crumble (see page 151)

1 quantity Ricotta Crème

Place a small saucepan over medium heat. Add the marsala or sweet desert wine, apple juice, vanilla bean and cinnamon and bring to the boil. Reduce heat to low.

Meanwhile, peel the pears and cut in half lengthwise. Using a teaspoon, scoop out the core. Add pears to the saucepan and simmer for 10 to 15 minutes or until tender. Test with a skewer. Remove pears and cinnamon stick with a slotted spoon and set aside.

Increase heat and reduce the syrup by half. Serve the poached pears topped with the syrup, Amaretti Crumble and a side serve of Ricotta Crème.

Ricotta crème

200 g (7 oz) fresh ricotta cheese

2 tablespoons natural yoghurt

½ teaspoon vanilla essence or seeds from ½ vanilla bean

1½ tablespoons icing (powdered) sugar

1 teaspoon lemon juice

Place all ingredients in a food processor and mix until smooth.

NOTE: Use ricotta crème as a substitute for whipped cream.

Vanilla yoghurt with passionfruit and amaretti crumble

1 treat

½ cup natural yoghurt

1 teaspoon manuka honey

2 passionfruit

2 tablespoons Amaretti Crumble (see page 151)

In a small bowl, mix the yoghurt and honey together. Pour into a small glass. Cut the passionfruit in half and scoop the pulp onto the yoghurt. Top with the Amaretti Crumble. Serve immediately.

NOTE: Mixed berries can be used as an alternative to the passionfruit.

Opposite page:
Vanilla yoghurt with passionfruit and amaretti crumble

Following pages:
Poached pears with amaretti crumble and ricotta crème

Chocolate berry tart with ricotta crème

8 slices

This is ideal for a celebration. It does not keep well because of the fresh ingredients so make it when you are feeding a number of people. Make the base and filling and put it together when you are about to serve it.

1½ cups rolled oats

2 tablespoons spelt flour, white or wholemeal

2 tablespoons Dutch cocoa

½ cup raw caster sugar

80 g (3 oz) butter, melted

½ cup rice or beans for blind baking

2 quantities Ricotta Crème (see page 152)

250 g (9 oz) small fresh strawberries, green tops removed, halved

200 g (7 oz) fresh raspberries

200 g (7 oz) fresh blueberries

icing (powdered) sugar for dusting

Preheat oven to 180°C (350°F). Grease a 34 x 11 cm (13 x 4 in) fluted tin.

Place the oats, flour, cocoa and sugar in a food processor and pulse for 20 seconds. Tip the mixture into a bowl and mix with the melted butter. Press the biscuit mixture into the prepared tin. Place a piece of baking paper over the base and tip rice or beans over top. This keeps the base flat while baking.

Bake in the oven for 15 minutes. Remove from oven and cool in tin then discard the rice or beans and baking paper. Remove very carefully from tin.

Fill with the ricotta crème and top with the strawberries, raspberries and blueberries. Dust with icing (powdered) sugar and serve immediately.

Almond and blueberry muffins

These muffins are denser than a muffin made with wheat flour, however they are delicious and satisfying because of the high-protein ingredients.

Makes 8–10

¾ cup spelt flour, white or wholemeal

1 teaspoon baking powder

¾ cup almond meal

¾ cup raw caster sugar

2 free-range or organic eggs, separated

pinch of Celtic sea salt

½ teaspoon vanilla essence

125 g (4.5 oz) butter, melted and cooled

1 cup fresh or frozen blueberries

icing (powdered) sugar for dusting

Preheat oven to 180°C (350°F). Line a 12-cup muffin pan with 10 muffin papers.

Sift the flour and baking powder into a large bowl and add the almond meal and sugar. Mix well.

Lightly whisk the egg yolks with the vanilla and add to the dry ingredients along with the melted butter. Mix well.

Whisk the egg whites with the Celtic salt until soft peaks form. Fold in the egg whites using a rubber spatula. Add the blueberries and stir gently to combine. The mixture is very thick.

Spoon into muffin papers until about two-thirds full and bake for 20 to 25 minutes. Cool slightly in tin before gently turning out. Dust with icing (powdered) sugar.

NOTE: Muffins can be frozen.

Ricotta chocolate mousse cake

10 slices

1 cup rolled oats
1 tablespoon spelt flour, white or wholemeal
3 tablespoons Dutch cocoa
1 cup raw caster sugar
55 g (2 oz) butter, melted
100 g (3.5 oz) dark chocolate, broken into pieces
600 g (21 oz) fresh ricotta cheese
½ teaspoon vanilla essence
3 free-range or organic eggs, lightly beaten
extra Dutch cocoa for dusting
250 g (9 oz) fresh raspberries

Grease and line a 20–22 cm (8–9 in) fluted or round spring-form tin.

Place the oats, spelt flour, 1 tablespoon of the Dutch cocoa and 1 tablespoon of the sugar in a food processor and pulse for 20 seconds. Tip the mixture into a bowl and mix with the melted butter. Press the biscuit mixture into the base of the prepared tin and place in the refrigerator to chill.

Preheat oven to 180°C (350°F).

Place a heatproof bowl over a saucepan of simmering water. Place the chocolate pieces in the bowl and melt gently.

Clean the bowl of the food processor then add the ricotta cheese, the remaining cocoa, sugar, vanilla essence, eggs and melted chocolate. Blend all ingredients until mixed and just smooth. Do not over mix. Pour into the biscuit base and loosely cover with a piece of foil. This prevents the top from cooking too quickly. Bake for 60 minutes.

Allow to cool completely before removing from the tin. Dust generously with extra cocoa and serve with fresh raspberries.

NOTE: This can be sliced into 10 portions and frozen.

Date and almond flan

8 slices

75 g (2.5 oz) butter, softened

75 g (2.5 oz) raw caster sugar

1 free-range or organic egg, beaten

$\frac{1}{2}$ teaspoon vanilla essence

75 g (2.5 oz) white spelt flour

$\frac{1}{2}$ teaspoon baking powder

100 g (3.5 oz) almond meal

12 fresh dates, pitted and sliced in half

2 tablespoons apricot fruit spread

Preheat oven to 180°C (350°F). Lightly grease a 20–22 cm (8–9 in) fluted loose-bottom flan tin.

Cream the butter and sugar together for a few minutes using an electric beater or food processor. Add the beaten egg and vanilla and mix well.

Sift the spelt flour and baking powder together and add to the butter mixture along with the almond meal. Mix until combined and spoon into the prepared flan tin. Spread evenly using a spatula; it is a sticky mixture.

Arrange the dates, cut side down, on top of the cake mixture. Bake for 20 to 25 minutes or until golden.

Meanwhile, warm the apricot spread in a small saucepan and brush it on top of the flan as soon as it comes out of the oven. Cool completely. Carefully remove the outside ring of the flan tin. Slice into portions and store in an airtight container for 7 days.

Cherry cheesecakes

These little cheesecakes can be frozen.

Makes 6–8

½ cup rolled oats
1 level tablespoon spelt flour, white or wholemeal
25 g (1 oz) butter, melted
½ cup raw caster sugar, plus 2 tablespoons extra
2 free-range or organic eggs, separated
¼ teaspoon vanilla essence or seeds from ½ vanilla bean
400 g (14 oz) fresh ricotta cheese, beaten until smooth
juice of ½ lemon
½ cup pitted cherries, drained
icing (powdered) sugar for dusting

Line a 12-cup muffin pan with 6–8 muffin papers. Place the oats, spelt flour and 2 tablespoons sugar in a food processor and pulse for 20 seconds. Tip the mixture into a bowl and mix with the melted butter. Press the biscuit mixture into the 6 or 8 muffin papers in the muffin pan and place in the refrigerator to chill for 10 minutes.

Preheat oven to 180°C (350°F).

Place ½ cup sugar and egg yolks in medium-sized bowl or food processor and beat well for 3 minutes. Add vanilla, ricotta and lemon juice and stir gently for 2 minutes.

In a small bowl, beat the egg whites until soft peaks form and gently fold into the cheesecake mix. Carefully fold the cherries through.

Pour the batter into the muffin papers over the biscuit bases and bake for 25 minutes or until golden. Allow the cheesecakes to cool slightly in the tin, remove and cool on a wire rack. Dust with icing (powdered) sugar.

Fruit and nut fudge

Makes 10 pieces

20 pitted dried dates
½ cup almonds, roughly chopped
¼ cup raisins, roughly chopped
150 g (5.5 oz) dark chocolate, roughly chopped
¼ teaspoon vanilla essence
butter or oil, for greasing
2 tablespoons flaked almonds

Place 15 dates in a food processor and pulse into a mushy ball. Set aside. Roughly chop the remaining 5 dates and place in a separate bowl with the almonds and raisins.

Fill a small saucepan halfway with water onto a medium heat. Place a heatproof bowl over the saucepan and add the chopped chocolate. Stir until melted. Add the vanilla and mushy dates and mix well. Pour the chocolate mixture into the bowl with chopped almonds, dates and raisins and stir to combine.

Lightly grease a 15 x 10 cm (6 x 4 in) plastic container with the butter or oil.

Spoon the mixture in, pressing firmly into the corners of the container. Sprinkle the top with the flaked almonds and press them into the mixture. Put the lid on the container and place in the refrigerator to cool for about 1 hour. Once cooled, turn the slab out onto a chopping board and slice into 10 pieces. Store in a plastic container.

NOTE: As an alternative, add 3 dried figs cut into smalll pieces or experiment with whatever nuts and dried fruit you may have in your pantry.

Raisin cookies

Makes 20-24

125 g (4.5 oz) butter, softened
¾ cup raw caster sugar
1 teaspoon vanilla essence
1 free-range or organic egg, beaten
1 cup white or wholemeal spelt flour
½ teaspoon baking powder
pinch of Celtic sea salt
1 cup rolled oats
1 cup raisins

Preheat the oven to 180°C (350°F) and line 2 trays with baking paper.

Use an electric mixer to beat the butter and sugar until pale and creamy. Add vanilla and egg and mix well.

Sift spelt flour with baking powder and a pinch of Celtic salt. Add to the butter mixture and when combined, stir in oats and raisins.

Flour the palm of your hand and roll heaped teaspoons of the mixture into balls. Place on trays, then flatten with a floured fork. The mixture is very sticky so you will need to re-flour your hands.

Bake for 12 to 15 minutes until golden brown. Allow to cool on trays for 5 minutes then transfer to a wire rack to cool completely. Keep in an airtight container for 10 days.

Bibliography

Books

Lust John B. 1959, *Raw Juice Therapy*, The Pitman Press, United Kingdom

Meyerowitz, Steve 1984, *Juice Fasting and Detoxification*, Sproutman Publications, United States

Farquharson Marie 1999 *Natural Detox,* Element Books Limited, United Kingdom

Brand Miller Jennie, Foster-Powell Kaye, Colagiuri Stephen, Leeds Anthony 1996, *The G.I. Factor: The Glucose Revolution*, Hodder Headline, Australia

Perricone Nicholas 2004, *The Perricone Promise*, Time-Warner Book Group, United States

Chopra Deepak 1990, *Perfect Health*, Bantam Books, United Kingdom

Lipski Elizabeth 1996, *Digestive Wellness,* Keats Publishing, United States

D'Adamo Peter 2001, *Live Right 4 Your Type*, Penguin Books, Australia

Lad Vasant 1999, *The Complete Book Of Ayurvedic Home Remedies*, Harmony Books, United Kingdom

Urs Koch Manfred 1981, *Laugh With Health*, Renaissance & New Age Creations, Australia

Journals

Chan JL, et al. Ghrelin levels are not regulated by recombinant leptin administration and/or three days of fasting in healthy subjects. J Clin Endocrinol Metab. 2004 Jan;89(1):335-43.

Epel ES, McEwen B, Seeman T, Matthews K, Castellazzo G, Brownell KD, Bell J, Ickovics JR., 'Stress and body shape: stress-induced cortisol secretion is consistently greater among women with central fat.', *Psychosom Med.* 2000 Sep-Oct;62(5):623-32

Di Marzo V, et al. Leptin-regulated endocannabinoids are involved in maintaining food intake. Nature. 2001 Apr 12;410(6830):822-5

Spiegel, K, Tasali, E, Penev, P and Van Cauter E. 2004, 'Sleep Curtailment in Healthy Young Men is Associated with Decreased Leptin Levels, Elevated Ghrelin Levels, and Increased Hunger and Appetite', *American College of Physicians*, 2004; 141 (11), pp846-851.

Tschop M, Weyer C, Tataranni PA, Devanarayan V, Ravussin E, Heiman ML., 'Circulating ghrelin levels are decreased in human obesity.', Diabetes. 2001 Apr;50(4):707

Wang MY, Orci L, Ravazzola M, Unger RH. 'Fat storage in adipocytes requires inactivation of leptin's paracrine activity: implications for treatment of human obesity', *Proc Natl Acad* Sci USA. 2005 Dec13;102(50):18011-16. Epub 2005 Dec 2.

Wren AM, Seal LJ, Cohen MA, Brynes AE, et al., 'Ghrelin enhances appetite and increases food intake in humans.', *J Clin Endocrinol Metab.* 2001 Dec; 86(12):5992.

Press releases

'Running slows the aging clock, Stanford researches find', Stanford School of Medicine Press Release, 11 August 2008

Index

ABOUT THE AUTHOR

Julie Rennie is an author and wellbeing speaker

In her bestselling book, *The Metabolic Clock*, Julie has inspired thousands of people to live a healthy, balanced lifestyle. Through her inspiring workshops she shows just how easy it is to change lifelong patterns and live your life to the full.

With a background as an elite athlete, a motivation coach to Olympic athletes and corporate trainer, Julie lives her life passionately, according to her own personal philosophy:

No matter what is happening in your life, it's important to be kind to yourself. When you are being loving, it's so much easier to take good care of yourself.

Julie is available for corporate events and gives book talks to community groups. You can contact Julie on her website.

For free downloads and workshop dates go to:
www.metabolicclock.com

Follow on Facebook:
http://www.facebook.com/TheMetabolicClock

- Are you struggling to lose weight no matter how hard you try?
- Do you feel exhausted at the end of each day?
- Is motivation and inspiration something you want to achieve?
- Are negative thoughts colouring the way you live your life?

Tap into the secrets of *The Metabolic Clock* and discover how you can speed up your metabolism easily, losing excess body fat without raising a sweat. Learn how to change those lifelong patterns that are preventing you from living life to the full. Ditch the diets, energise your mind and body, live the healthy and positive life you deserve.

Another inspirational book from Rockpool Publishing

ROCKPOOL
PUBLISHING

www.rockpoolpublishing.com.au